Piano & Keyboard Performance For The Beginner

by Adrian Bynoe

ISBN 978-976-8265-56-2

Copyright © 2017   All Rights Reserved   Made and Printed in Barbados

No part of this publication may be reproduced in any form or by any means
without the prior written permission of the Publisher

Contents

Page

Chapter 1: The Keyboard Family 1

Chapter 2: Keyboard Familiarization 3
    Names of the White Keys 4
    Names of the Black Keys 4
    Familiarization Test 6

Chapter 3: Theory of Music 7
    The Stave 7
    Ledger Lines 8
    Notes and Their Values 8
    Time Signatures 10
    Dots and Ties 11
    Key Signatures 12
    Circle of Fourths & Fifths 14

Chapter 4: The Construction of Major Chords and Major Scales 15
    Major Scales 16
    Major Chords 17

Chapter 5: Major Scales, Major Chords and Exercises 18
    C Major 19
    G Major 24
    D Major 29
    A Major 34
    E Major 39
    B Major 44
    F Major 49
    B♭ Major 54
    E♭ Major 59
    A♭ Major 64
    D♭ Major 69
    G♭ Major 74

Chapter 6: Families of Chords 79

Chapter 7: Playing Songs 82
    Jesus Loves Me 83
    Rock-A-Bye Baby 84
    Old MacDonald 85
    Love Lifted Me 86

Practice Schedule 88

Chapter 1
The Keyboard Family

A harpsichord is a musical instrument played by means of a keyboard. When the player presses one or more key, this triggers a mechanism, which plucks one or more strings with a small quill. This concept was derived from an instrument called the Harp. The harpsichord was most probably invented in the late Middle Ages (5th - 15th Century)

Harpsichord

Grand Piano

Upright Piano

The piano is an acoustic, stringed musical instrument invented around the year 1700 (the exact year is uncertain), in which the strings are struck by hammers. It is played using a keyboard. The word piano is a shortened form of Pianoforte, the Italian term for the early 1700s versions of the instrument. Modern Pianos have 88 keys.

Digital pianos produce a variety of piano timbres and other sounds. For example, a digital piano may have settings for a Concert Grand Piano, an Upright Piano, etc. Some also incorporate other basic 'Synthesizer' sounds such as String Ensemble, Woodwinds and Brass for example, and offer settings to combine them with a Piano sound.

Digital Piano

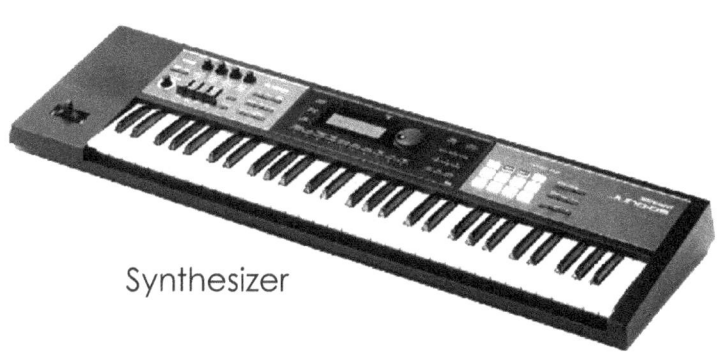
Synthesizer

A synthesizer is an electronic musical instrument that generates electric signals that are converted to sound. Synthesizers may either imitate instruments like the Piano, Hammond Organ, Flute, Trumpet, Trombone, Violin, Harp, Guitar, Bass, Drums, Strings, other unnatural sounds and even vocals.

Workstation

A Workstation is the combination of a Music Sequencer and a Synthesizer which originated in the late 1970s. Control devices such as musical keyboards became feasible to combine into a single piece of equipment that was affordable to high-end studios and producers, as well as being portable for performers.

Modern Synthesizers and other types of Electronic Keyboards are manufactured in different sizes. The keyboards mainly comprise 49, 61, 76 and 88 Keys. These numbers are a total of black and white keys, with the 49key Keyboard having four octaves, 61key Keyboard having five octaves, 76key Keyboard having six octaves and the 88key Keyboard having seven octaves.

• • • • • • • •

I recommend that you purchase either an Acoustic Piano, Electronic Piano or a Keyboard with 88 weighted keys. A sales clerk at a music store will be able to point you in the right direction.

There are many good brands available. Some good brands of Electronic Pianos and Keyboards are **Roland**, **Yamaha**, and **Korg**. If these brands are out of your budget you can also choose a **Casio** brand.

To get the best results from this course, read all information and instructions thoroughly. Do not rush the course, practice and study 5 days a week for a minimum of 30 minutes.

If you follow the suggested Schedule, located at the back of this book (Page 88), you will be able to play at an intermediate level in 16 weeks.

Chapter 2
Keyboard Familiarization

The first thing you need to know before you begin to play is the design of the Piano/Keyboard. The keys are arranged in a particular form and they can be identified easily once that pattern is learnt.

Diagram 1

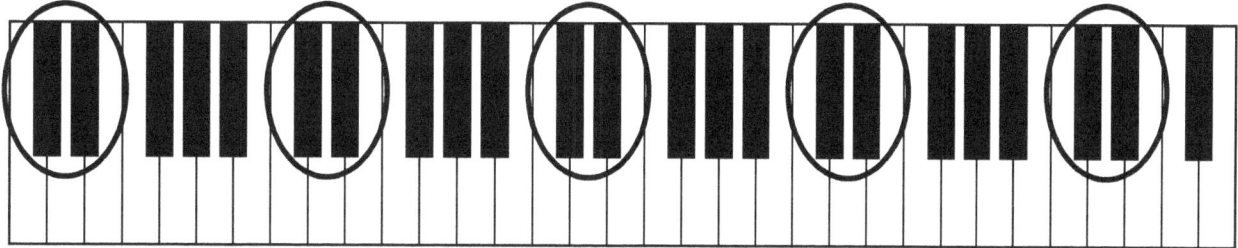

There is a repeated pattern of the group of 2 Black Keys

Diagram 2

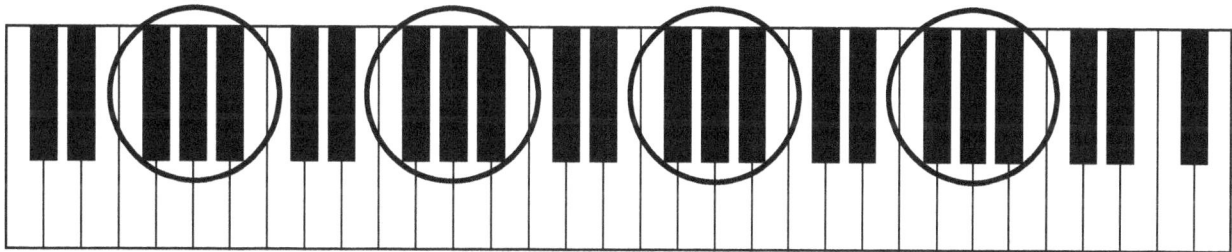

There is also a repeated pattern of the group of 3 Black Keys

It is important to be aware of the pattern and arrangement of the keys on the Keyboard. The following exercises will assist you greatly with recognizing the keys and their names. I advise that you spend adequate time on familiarizing yourself with the key names.

Keyboard Familiarization

* Use the pointer finger on either of your hands in the exercises.

Names of the White Keys

'**C**' is on the left side of the group of 2 black keys.

'**E**' is on the right side of the group of 2 black keys.

'**F**' is on the left side of the group of 3 black keys.

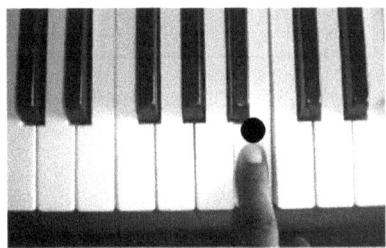
'**B**' is on the right side of the group of 3 black keys.

'**D**' is in the centre of the group of 2 black keys.

'**G**' is inside of the group of 3 black keys.

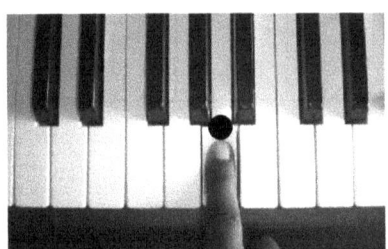
'**A**' is inside of the group of 3 black keys.

Names of the Black Keys

Each black key has two names and one of the names will be referred to depending on the scale it is being used in. For example, the black key called '**C#**' in the '**A**' major scale is also '**D♭**' in the '**A♭**' major scale. More of this theory will be explained as we go along in this book.

Keyboard Familiarization

Diagram 3

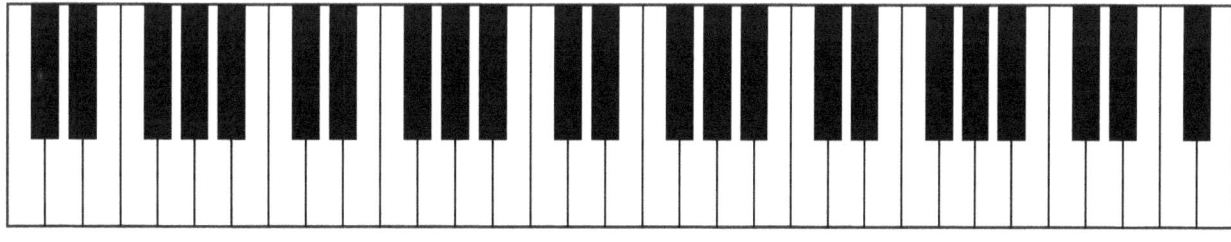

Pitch Ascending →

If you play each key, black and white in a left to right direction you will recognize that the pitch or sound of each note gets higher or 'sharper'.

Diagram 4

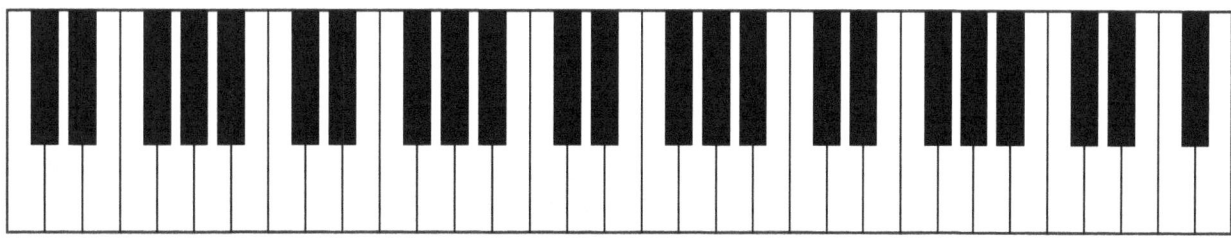

← *Pitch Descending*

If you play each key, black and white in a right to left direction you will recognize that the pitch or sound of each note gets lower or 'flatter'.

A black key gets its names from the white keys around it.
e.g *The black key to the right of '***C***' is higher or sharper therefore it is called '***C#***'.* ***(C Sharp)*** *the same black key is to the left of '***D***' and is lower or flatter than '***D***' and it is also called '***D♭***' (**D Flat**)*

C#/ D♭

D#/ E♭

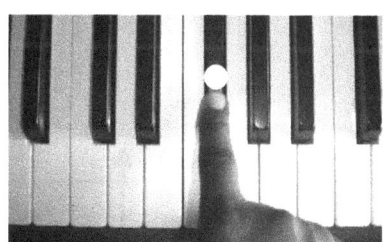

F#/ G♭

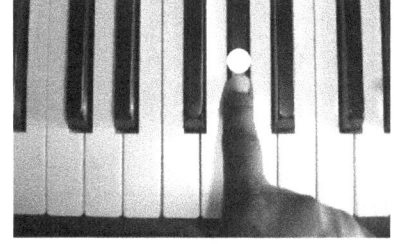

G#/ A♭

A#/ B♭

Keyboard Familiarization Test

If you think that you can remember the names of the keys on the keyboard, it's time to take this test. Fill in the blank lines under each keyboard diagram with the key names. ***There are 3 extra test sheets supplied for you to re-test yourself as many times as you like.*** Use a clock to time yourself, the faster you get it filled out, the more familiar you are with the keyboard. *(Use a pencil to fill in the blanks)*

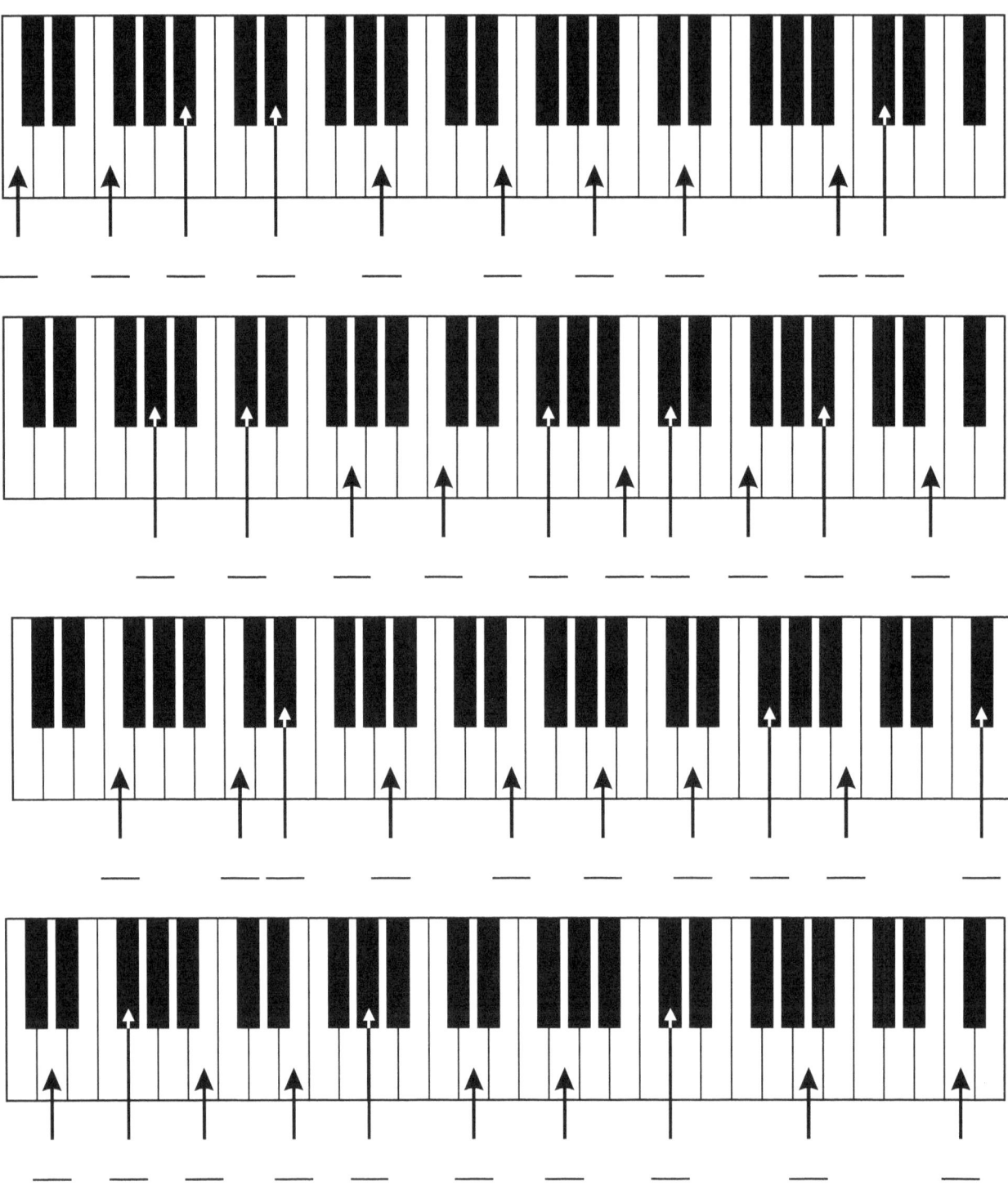

Chapter 3

Theory of Music

Music is a language! Like any other language such as English, Spanish, etc. it is important to do more than just listen and speak it (in this case, play it). You should be able to read it. Although this is a learning to play by 'Ear' course, I think that it is necessary to help you learn and understand basic Music Theory.

Musical sounds are called notes, which are named after the first seven letters of the Alphabet. { **A. B. C. D. E. F. G.** }

The Stave/Staff

The Stave or Staff is a set of five horizontal lines and four spaces that each represent a different musical pitch. In some cases they can represent different percussion instruments. Suitable music symbols are placed on the Stave/Staff according to their corresponding pitch or function. Musical notes are placed by pitch, percussion notes are placed by instrument, and rests and other symbols are placed as needed.

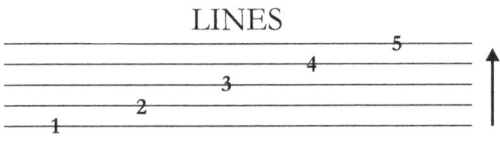

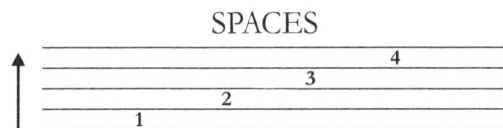

The lines are numbered from bottom to top

The spaces are numbered from bottom to top

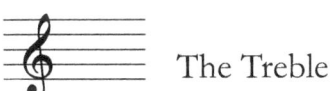 The Treble Clef

The symbol on the Stave above is called the Treble Clef. When placed on the Stave, it indicates that the notes should be played with the right hand unless otherwise instructed and it dictates what the names of the notes should be.

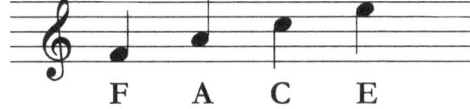

 The Bass Clef

The symbol on the Stave above is called the Bass Clef. When placed on the Stave, it indicates that the notes should be played with the left hand unless otherwise instructed and it dictates what the names of the notes should be.

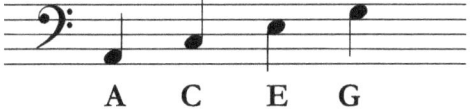

Theory of Music

Ledger Lines

A Ledger Line or Leger Line is used to write pitches above or below the Stave. It is a line that is slightly longer than the note head drawn parallel to the Stave, above or below, spaced at the same distance as the lines within the Stave.

Each note on the Stave indicates a particular key on the Keyboard/Piano. To be precise, an '**A**', '**C**' or '**F**', etc. written on the Stave is not just any '**A**', '**C**' or '**F**' note on the Keyboard, it is indicating which key is to be played.

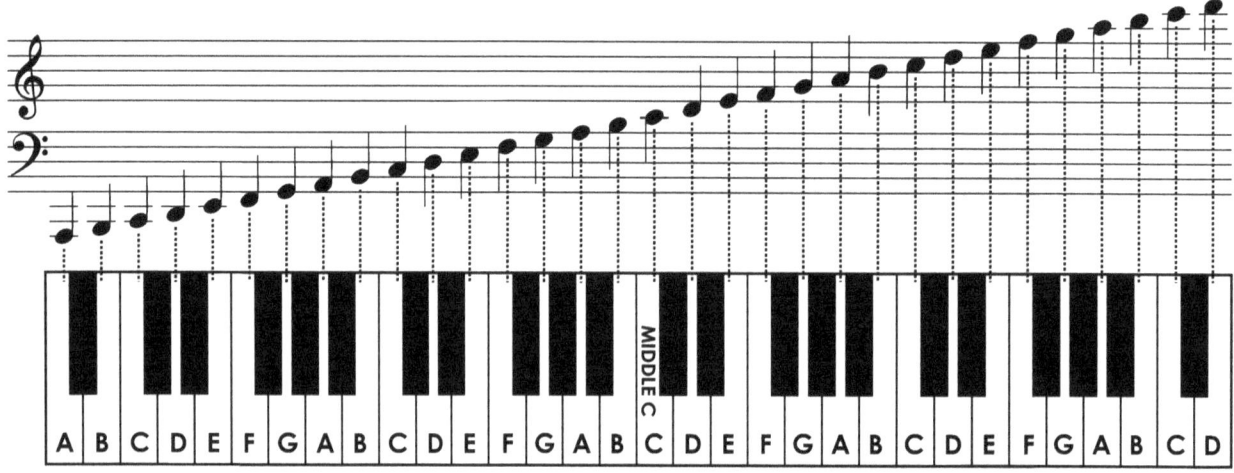

Notes & Their Values

Music is not only expressed in pitch. Rhythm plays just as important a role as sound. Imagine playing a musical piece without any rhythm. They are different types of written notes which control the rhythm.

Theory of Music

Rhythm is a strong, regular, repeated pattern of movement or sound and should not be mistaken for tempo. Rhythm can also be described as a pulse. Let's begin with these four notes to explain the basic concept of rhythm. There are other notes and symbols that assist with rhythm arrangement.

Each note requires one sound but its type indicates the duration of the sound or how long the sound should be held.

𝐨 - **Semibreve** (Whole Note)

The Whole note is the reference note for all the other notes

The note is to be sounded once and held for four beats.

𝅗𝅥 - **Minim** (Half Note)

The note is to be sounded once and held for two beats.

♩ - **Crotchet** (Quarter Note)

The note is to be sounded once and held for one beat.

♪ - **Quaver** (Eighth Note)

The note is to be sounded once and held for half of a beat.

<u>**1**</u>   <u>**2**</u>   <u>**3**</u>   <u>**4**</u>

Theory of Music

Time Signatures

Short upright lines drawn through the Stave are called **Bar Lines**, which divide music into equal portions of time. These lines separate beats into groups called **Bars** or **Measures**.

At the beginning of musical pieces there are signs placed to indicate the time and rhythm, these signs are called **Time Signatures**. I will introduce two time signatures at this point which are the two most commonly used in music.

This sign is called **Four-Four**. This means that there are four Crotchets or the equivalent in each Bar.

Each Bar has the equivalent of four Crotchets. Below are a few examples.

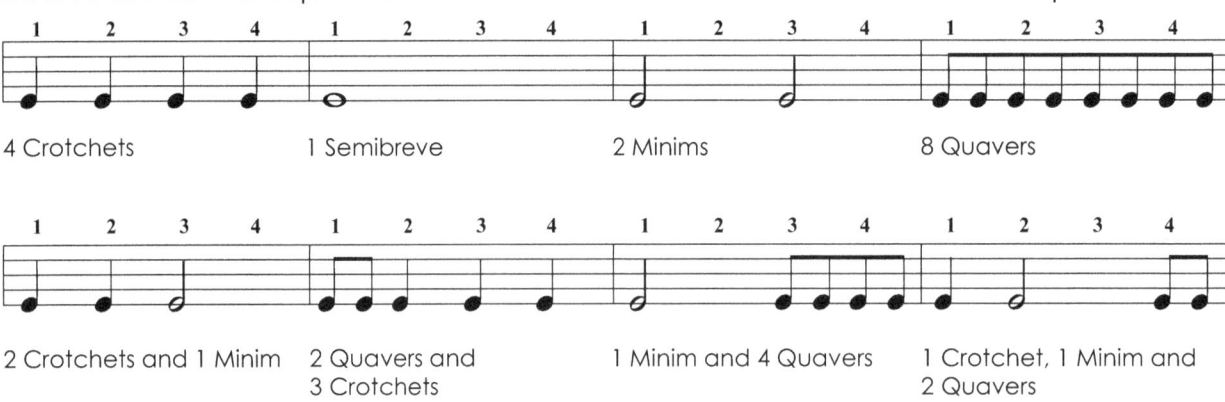

This sign is called **Three-Four**. This means that there are three Crotchets or the equivalent in each Bar.

Each Bar has the equivalent of three Crotchets. Below are a few examples.

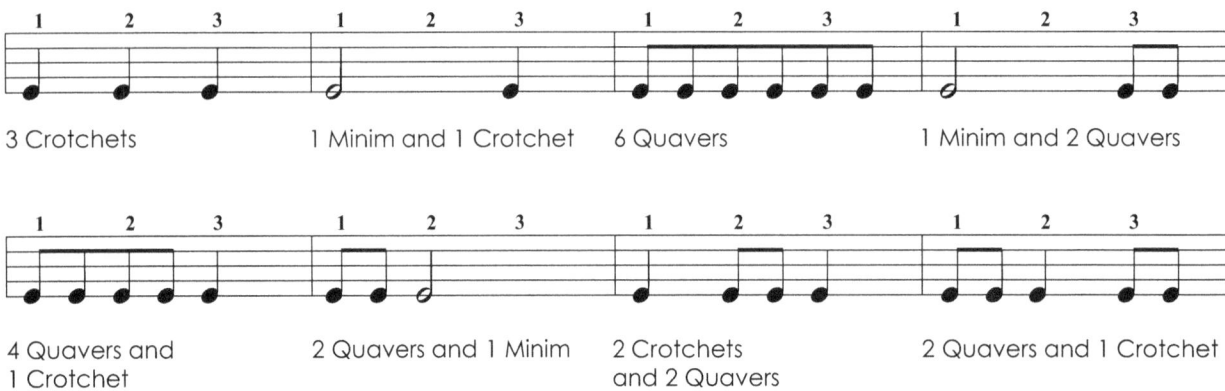

Theory of Music

Dots & Ties

Some notes need to be played and held for more than 4 beats, 2 beats, 1 beat, etc. There are no notes used in written music to represent a note that needs to be held for 3 beats. This is where Dots come in. A Dot increases the duration of a single note.

Dots increase the value of a note by half its value.

Example 1

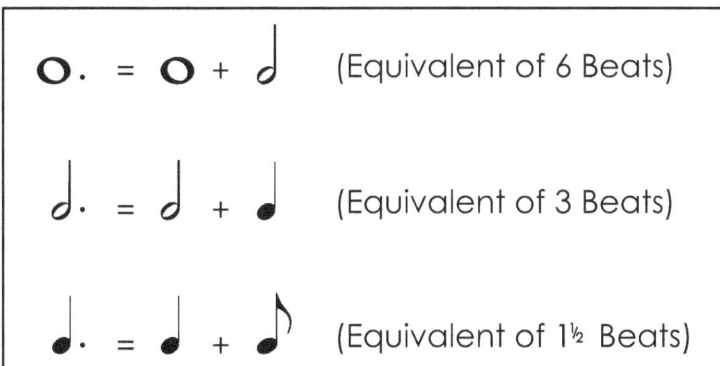

A Tie is used mostly when the value of a note causes it to go over the bar line and exceed the measure's value, or in place of a dotted note that is having the same issue. If a musical piece is in 4/4 timing and there is a measure that has three quarter notes, and one dotted quarter note, this would cause the dotted note to exceed the measure by an eighth note (*half the value of the quarter note*). In this instance we would replace the dotted quarter note with a normal quarter note, and tie it to an eighth note in the next measure. A Tie looks like a 'Slur' but is used differently. Slurs will be explained further in the Intermediate Book.

Example 1

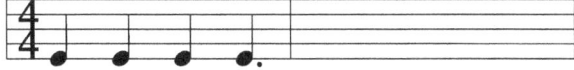   

The time is 4/4, so there can not be 4 and a half beats in the measure

The tie is used to extend the duration of the half beat to the next measure.

Example 2

A Tie should be used on the heads of the notes and not the tails.

A Tie should be used on notes with the same pitch.

11

Theory of Music

Key Signatures

At the beginning of musical pieces there are signs also placed to indicate the Key, these signs are called **Key Signatures**. Different songs are composed in different keys and it is important to know in which key a piece is to be played by recognizing the sign given.

The key is indicated by Sharps or Flats. You should remember those terms from Chapter 2.

♯ - **Sharp** (This sign raises a note by a Semi Tone)

♭ - **Flat** (This sign lowers a note by a Semi Tone)

Let's take a look at the key of **A Major**. Refer to all the information given so far and use it to better understand the diagram below.

Diagram 1

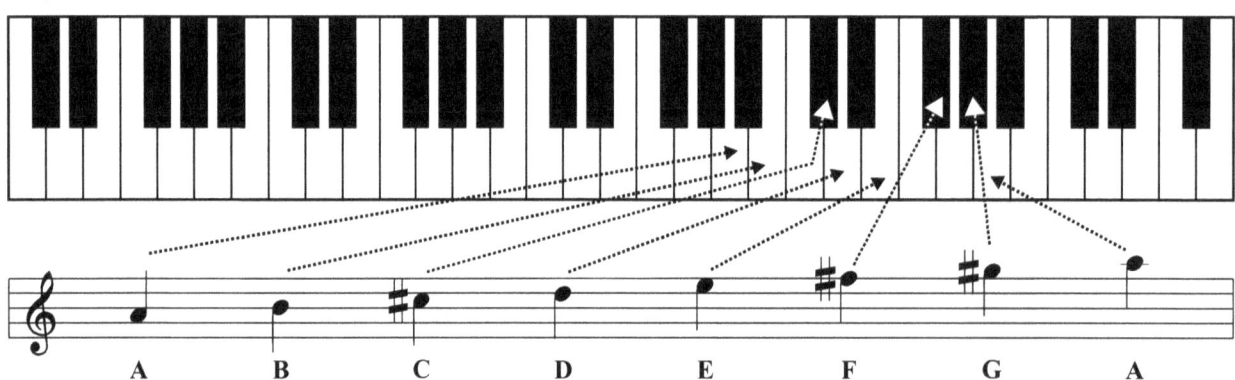

Diagram 2

 The Key Signature for **A Major** is a group of three Sharps.

The number of Sharps or Flats is not the only thing to recognize, it is helpful to be aware of where they are placed. If you look at **Diagram 1** above, you will see three notes with Sharps next to them, the notes are **C**, **F** and **G** and these three notes are to be 'sharpened' or raised. If these notes are played as natural **C**, **F** and **G**, then the scale would be wrong, the intervals need to be correct. If natural **C** is played, then the interval between the **2nd** and **3rd** notes would be incorrect and the same for the interval between the **3rd** and **4th** notes. The notes played then should be **C♯**, **F♯**, and **G♯**. You should also see where the notes are on the Stave. In the third space is **C**, on the fifth line is **F** and **G** sits on the top of the Stave, therefore the sharps are placed in the same positions on the Stave to indicate the three sharpened notes in the **A Major** scale.

12

Theory of Music

The diagrams below give you a quick reference to all the Key Signatures.
Try to memorize them as best as you can.

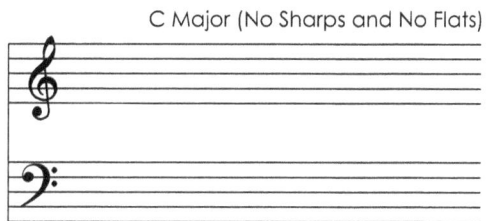

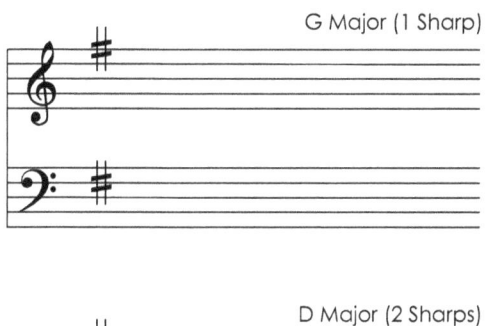

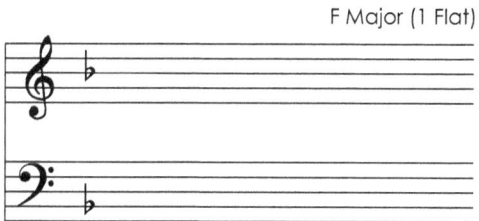

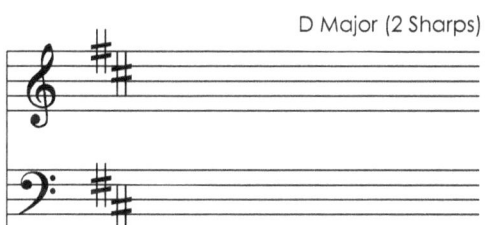

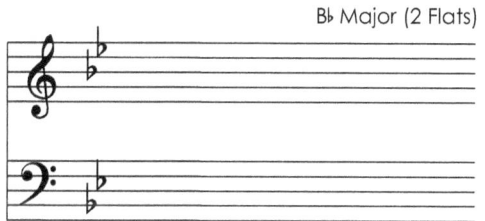

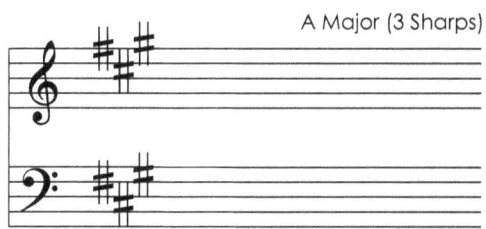

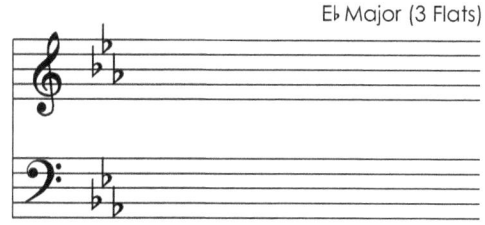

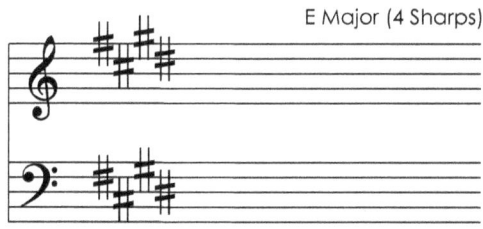

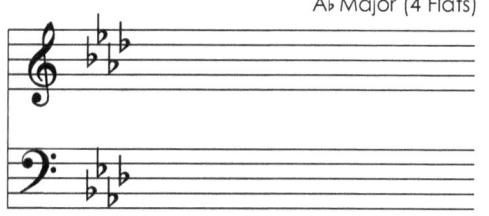

13

Theory of Music

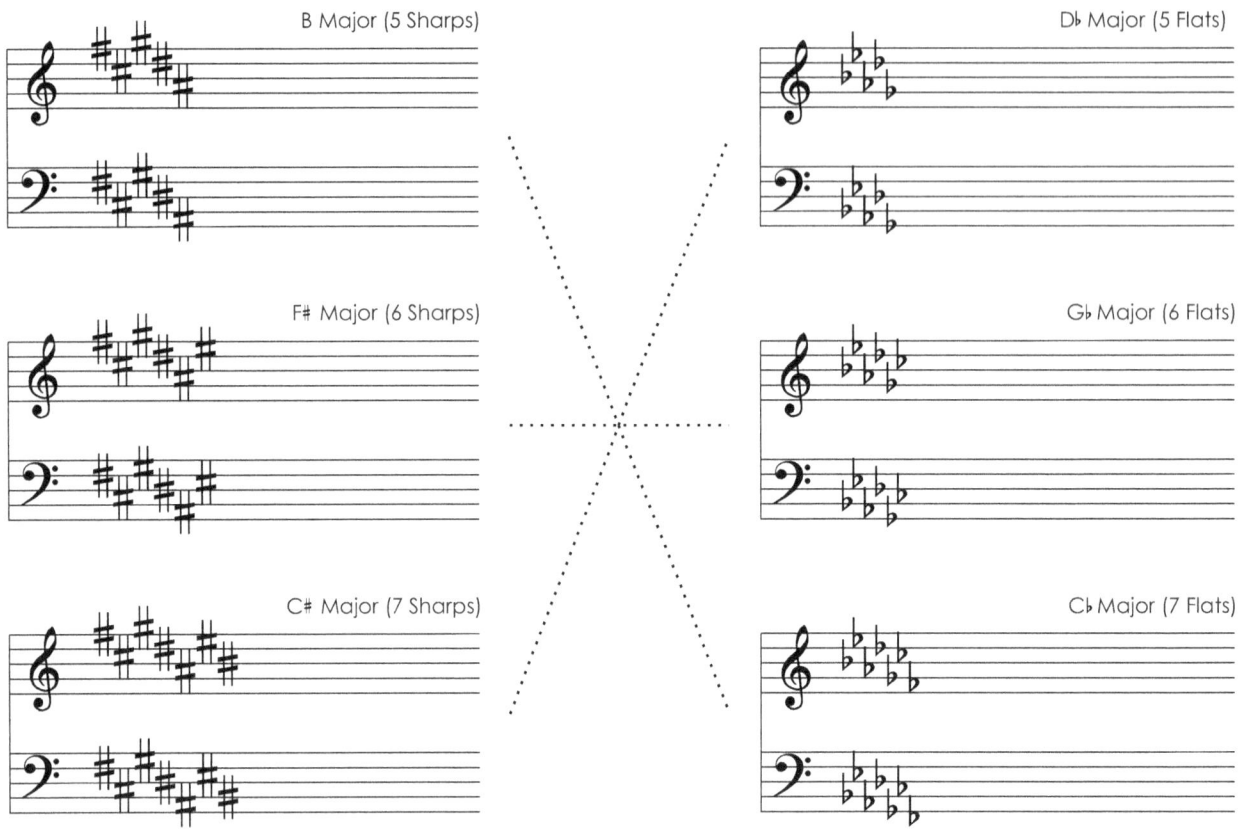

The dotted lines join the keys which are equivalents

The sequence of sharps and flats can also be seen in the diagram below. If it is read clockwise, each key has one sharp more and is five notes higher. If it is read anti-clockwise, each key has one flat more and is four notes higher.

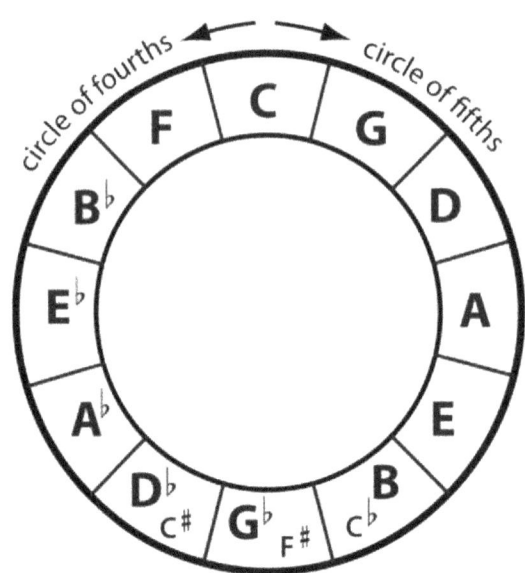

Chapter 4

The Construction of Major Scales and Major Chords

I previously indicated to you that if each black and white key is played in a left to right direction, that you would hear the pitch or sound getting higher and if played in a right to left direction, that the pitch or sound would get lower. While carrying out those exercises there is another concept that you should be made aware of and that is the distances or Intervals between each note. An Interval is the difference or distance between two notes. If you played each black and white key in a left to right direction, the pitch would be ascending in Half or Semi tones. If you played each black and white key in a right to left direction, the pitch would be descending in Half or Semi tones. Therefore the interval or distance between each note played ascending or descending, is a Half Tone or Semi Tone.

Diagram 1

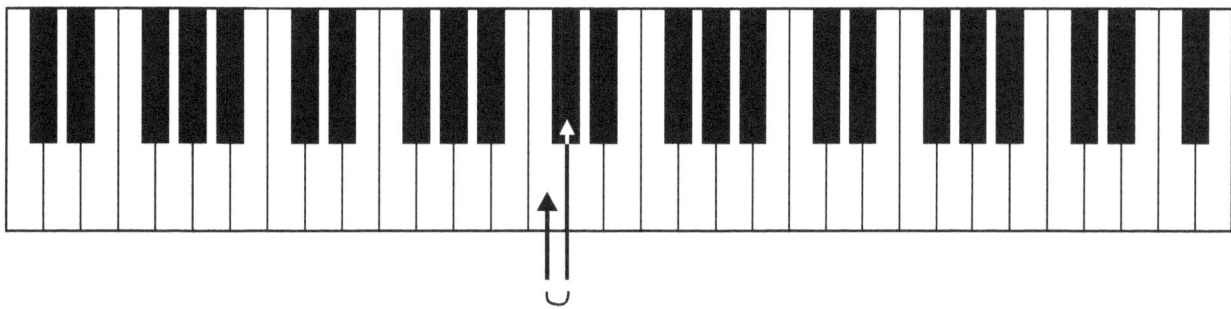

Example 1
The interval between '**C**' and '**C#/Db**' is a Semi Tone, in other words, they are a Semi Tone or Half Tone apart.

If you play '**C**', '**C#**' and '**D**' in progression, you would have ascended by two Semi Tones. If you add two halves together, the total would be a 'Whole'. Therefore, two Semi or Half tones make a Whole Tone or as it is also called, a 'Tone'.

Diagram 2

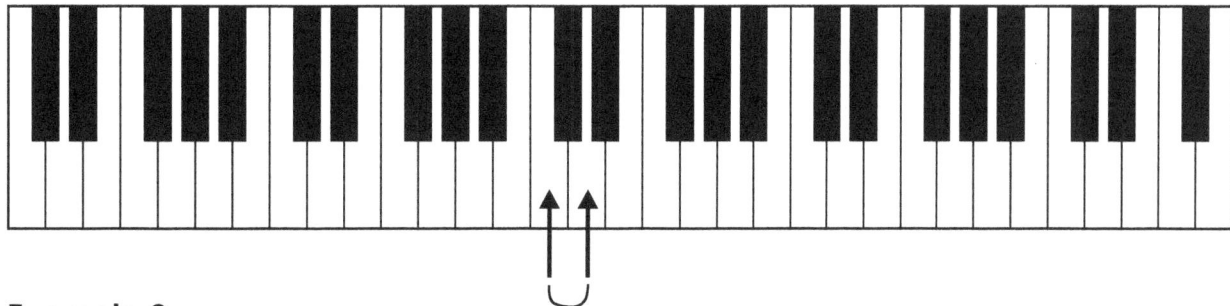

Example 2
The interval between '**C**' and '**D**' is a whole tone, in other words, they are a whole tone or a tone apart.

15

Construction of Major Scales and Chords

If you play '**C**', '**C#**', '**D**' and '**D#**' in progression, you would have ascended by three Semi Tones. If you add three halves together, the total would be 'One and a Half'. Therefore, three Semi or Half tones make a 'Tone and a Half'.

Diagram 3

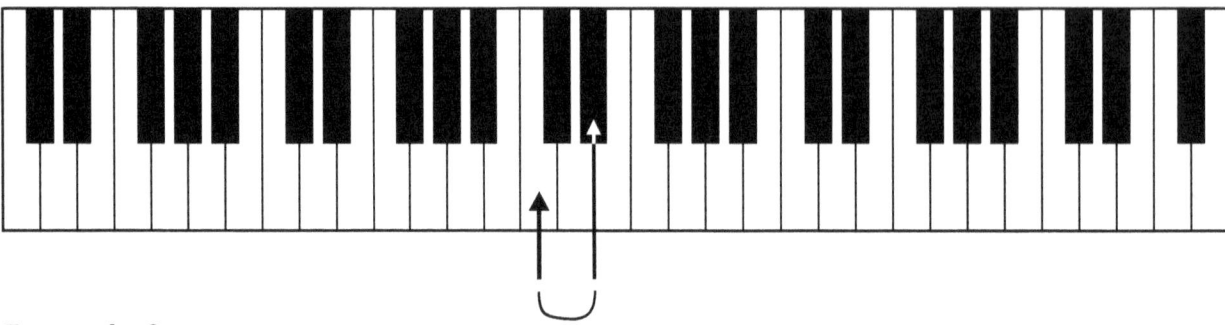

Example 3
The interval between '**C**' and '**D#/E♭**' is a Tone and a Half, in other words, they are a Tone and a Half apart.

Major Scales

There are four rules for constructing a Major Scale

1. The scale must begin and end with the same note name. If the name of the first note is 'C', the name of the last note must be 'C'.

2. The scale must consist eight (8) notes.

3. The notes must be in alphabetical order and no name should occur twice. E.g - When the C Major Scale is written, there should be only one D, F, A, etc.

4. Each note should have an interval of a Whole Tone except between the third and fourth notes and the seventh and eighth notes.

Example 4

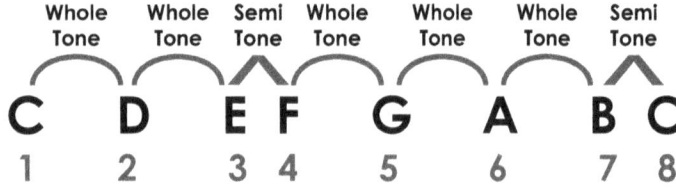

An interval of a whole tone is between **C&D**, **D&E**, **F&G**, **G&A** and **A&B**, while an interval of a Semi Tone is between **E&F and B&C**.

16

Construction of Major Scales and Chords

Major Chords

A Chord is a set of two or more notes sounded or played simultaneously (at the same time). A Major Chord is made up of three notes which is also called a Triad. The Major Chord consist of the first, third and fifth notes of a Major Scale.

Diagram 1

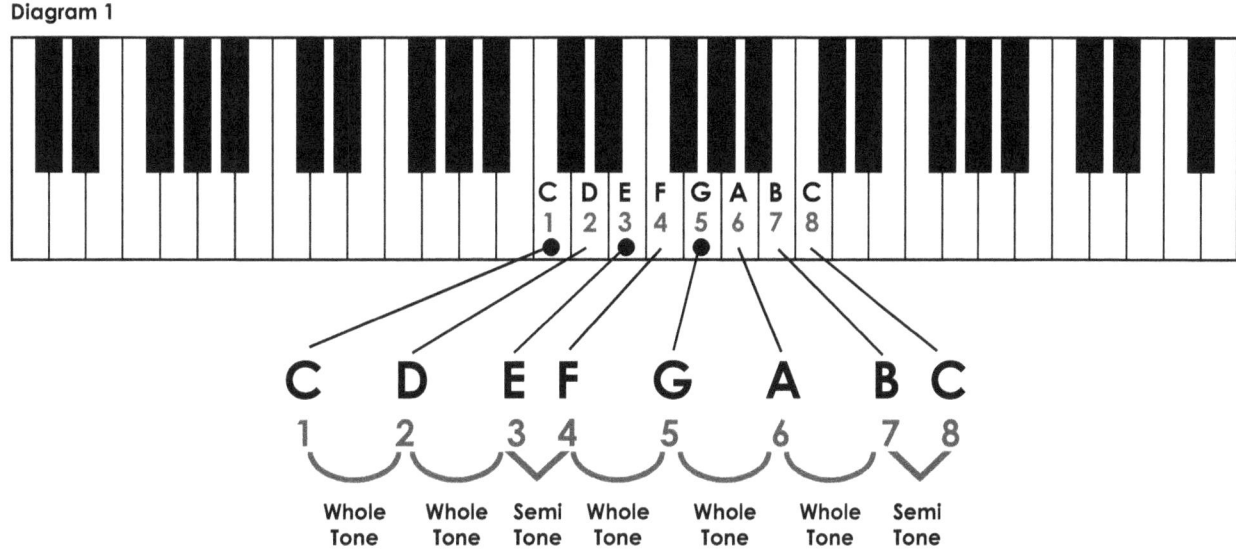

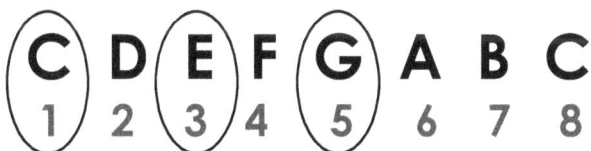

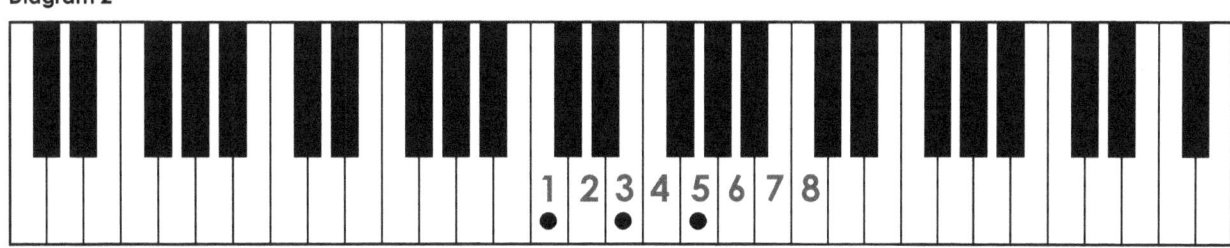

Diagram 2

Chapter 5

Major Scales, Major Chords & Exercises

Exercise Tips

READ THESE TIPS REGULARLY

Before you start the exercises some preparation needs to be done and there are other things you will need to know.

* Correct fingering should be used when playing scales.
* A Metronome should be used. - (*Contact a music store for assistance*)
* Start with a moderate tempo. Don't try to go too fast.
* The Exercises are in **Four-Four** timing
* Repeat one exercise many times before going on to another.

This is the numbering for the fingers of both hands.

The numbers placed above the notes indicate the finger with which the note should be played.

Before attempting the two-handed exercises, you should be able to play the scale fluently with each hand.

Root Position - When the note that represents the name of the chord (also called the root note) is the lowest note of the chord, that chord is being held in the root position.

Do not play chords in the lower register of the keyboard. If this is done you will hear a 'muddy' quality. It is advised that the notes be played further apart or single as you play in the lower register.

METRONOME TEMPO
Increase the tempo as you get more comfortable with playing the scale.

076

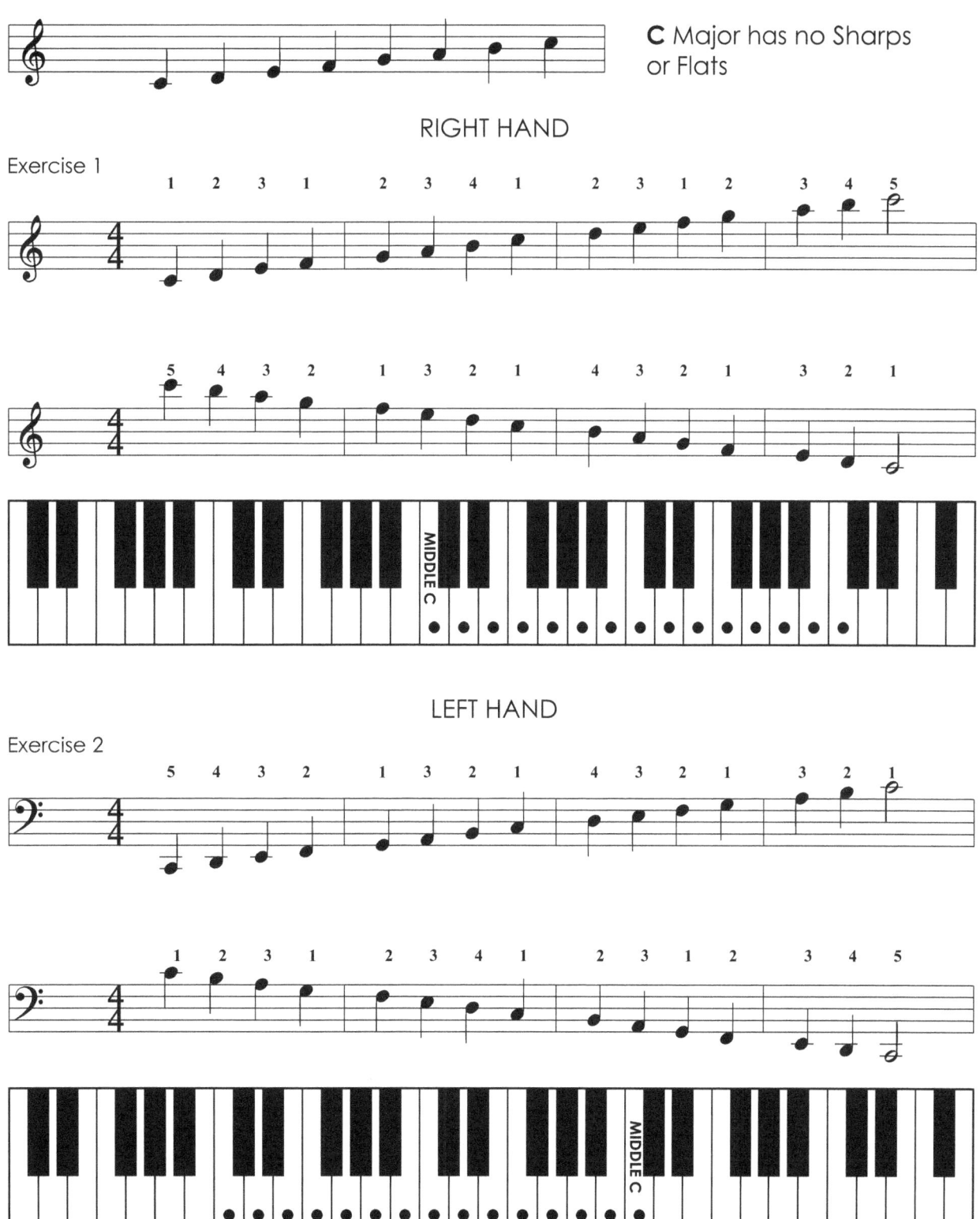

Major Scales, Major Chords & Exercises - C Major

BOTH HANDS

Exercise 3

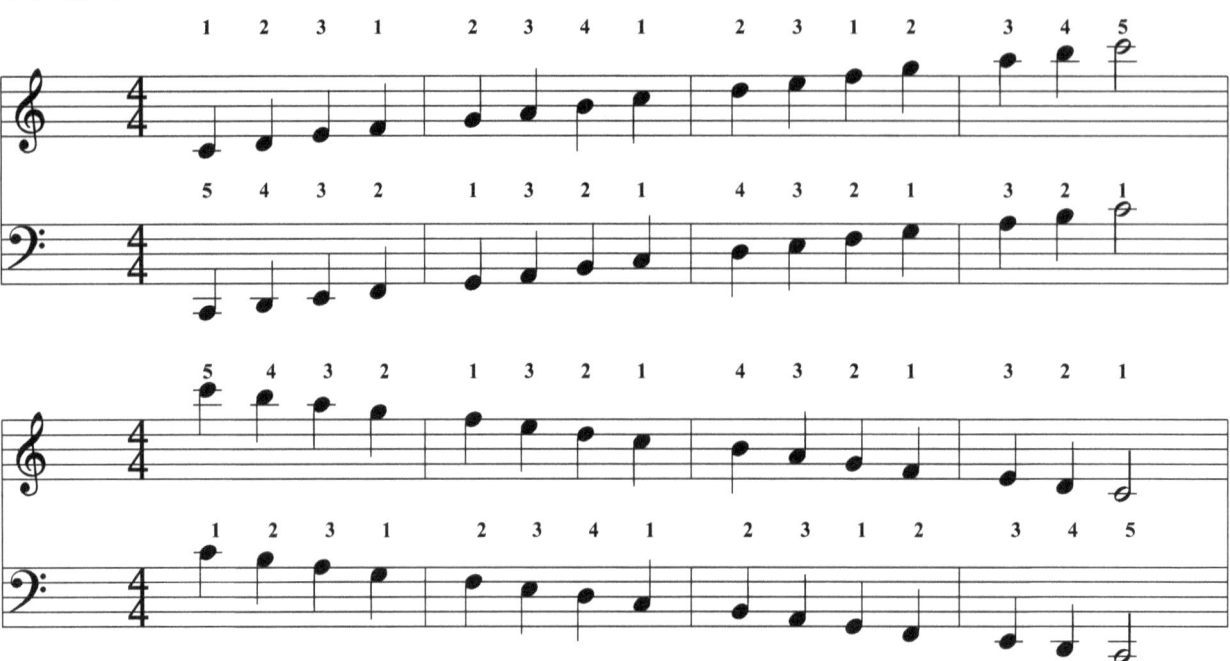

The Chord

The written symbol for the C Major chord is '**C**Maj'.

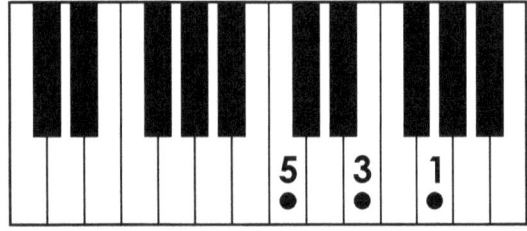

The Left Hand holding **C Major** chord with numbers 5, 3 and 1 fingers.

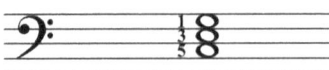

The **C Major** chord written on the Stave (Bass Clef).

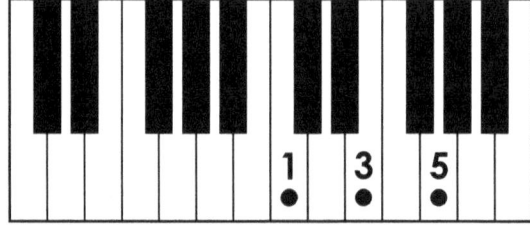

The Right Hand holding **C Major** chord with numbers 1, 3 and 5 fingers.

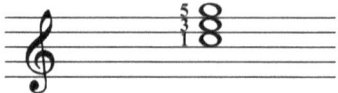

The **C Major** chord written on the Stave (Treble Clef).

Major chords can be played in three different positions. These positions are called Inversions. It is not always possible to hold an inverted chord with numbers 1, 3 and 5 fingers, numbers 2 or 4 fingers may be substituted as needed.

Major Scales, Major Chords & Exercises - C Major

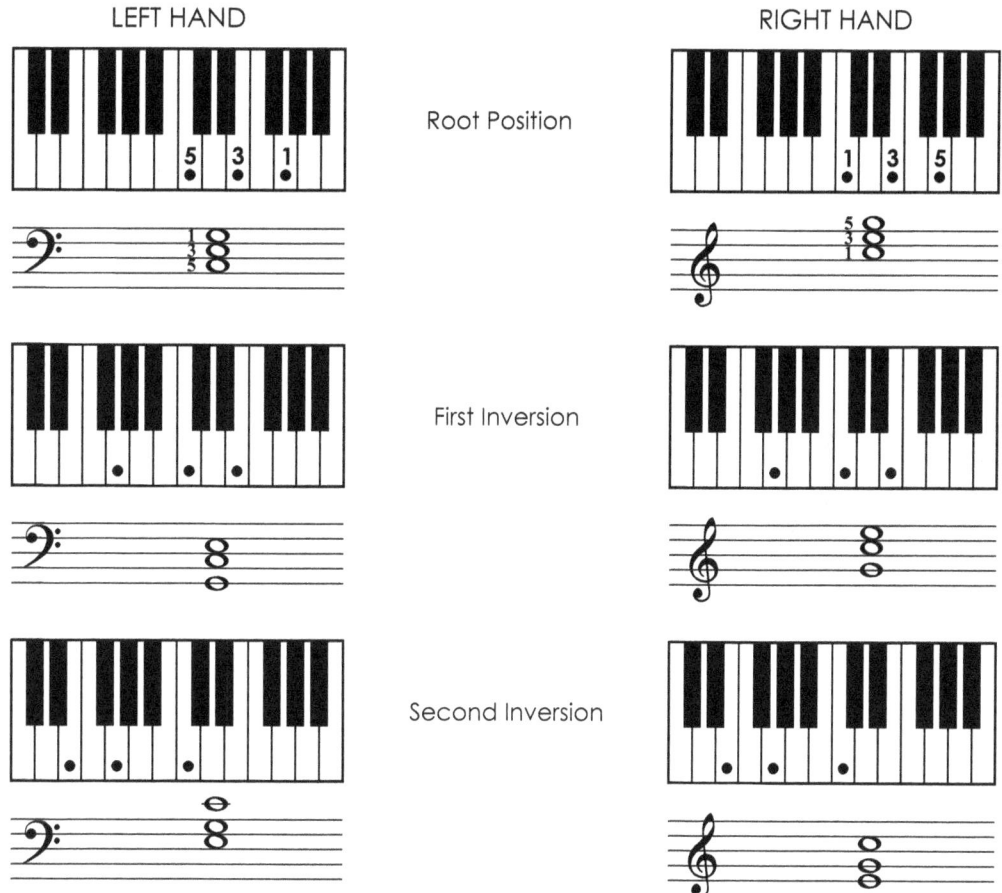

The two pictures below give examples of using both hands to play a chord. The two hand method produces a full or rich sound. Another purpose for the two hand method is to allow the hands to function in separate capacities. For example, the right hand can hold a chord while the left hand plays a pattern or the left hand can hold a chord while the right hand plays a melody, etc.

BOTH HANDS

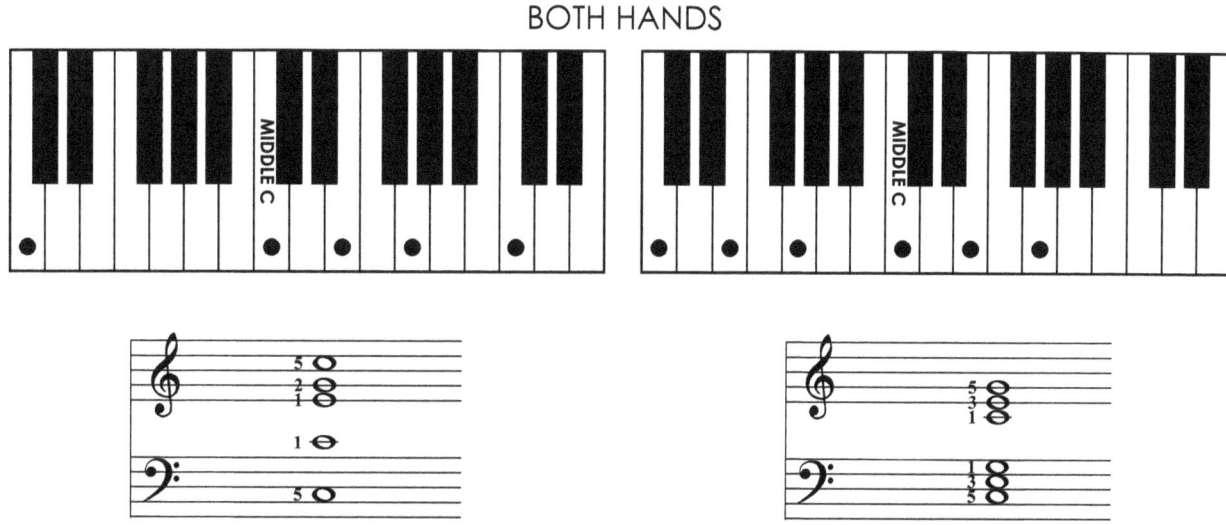

Major Scales, Major Chords & Exercises - *C Major*

Exercise 1

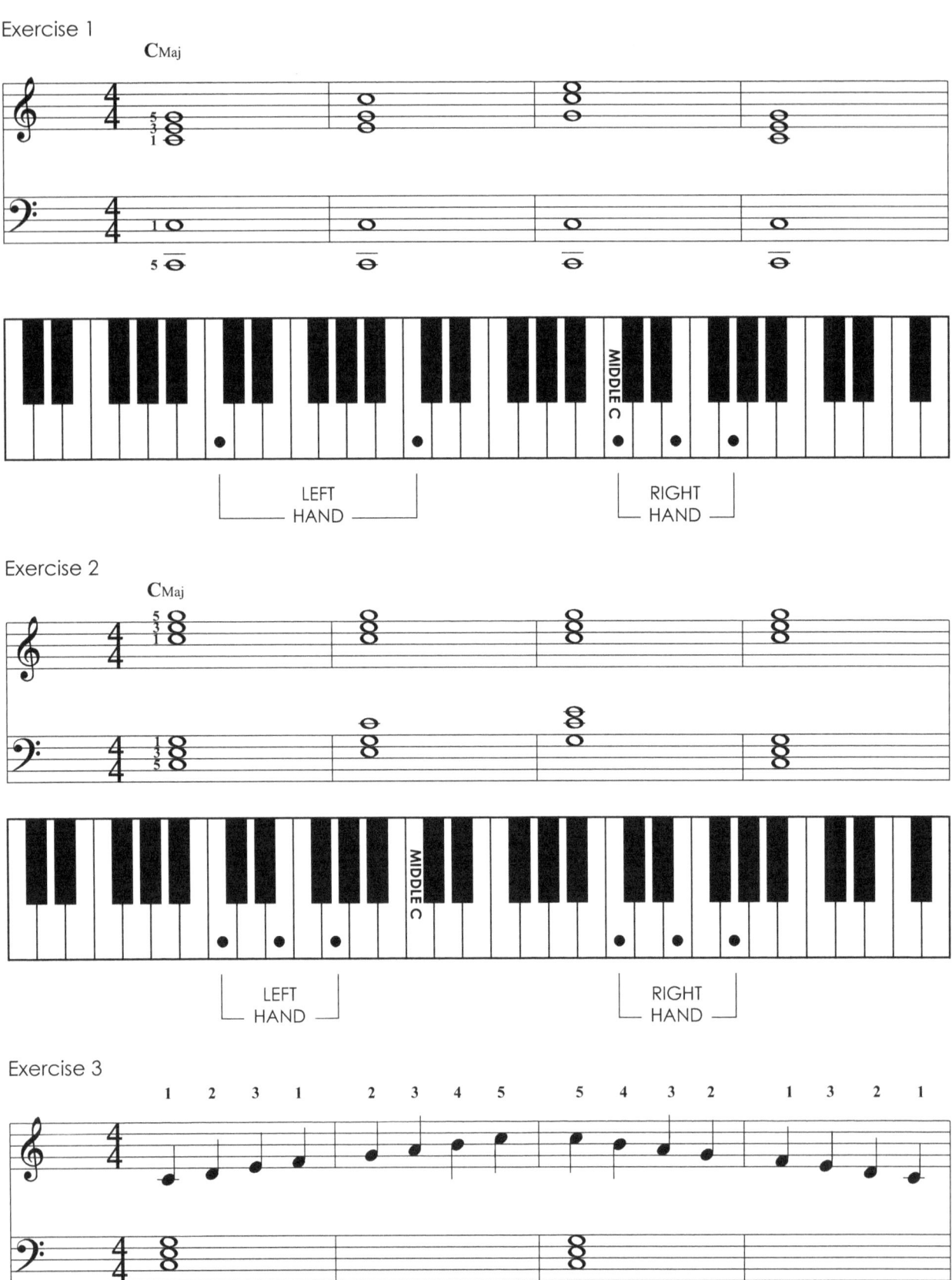

Exercise 2

Exercise 3

Major Scales, Major Chords & Exercises - *C Major*

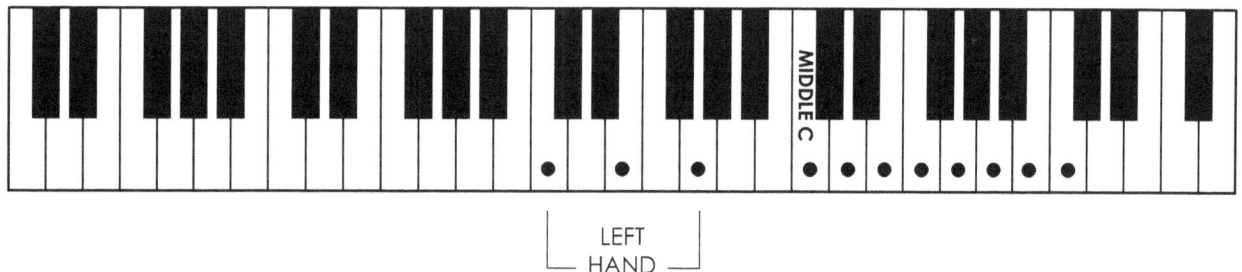

Exercise 4

Exercise 5

Exercise 6

The Key of G Major

The Scale

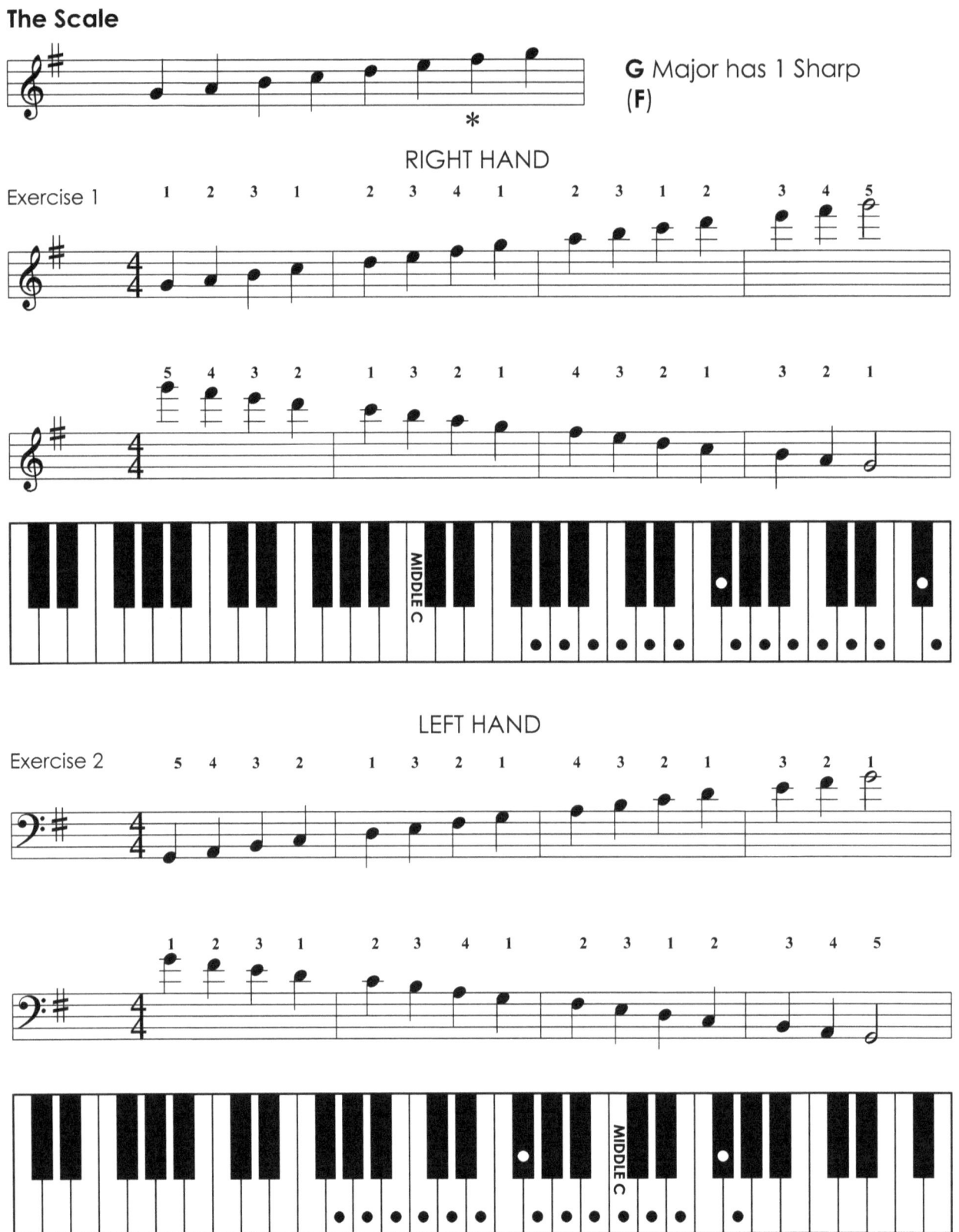

G Major has 1 Sharp (**F**)

RIGHT HAND

Exercise 1

LEFT HAND

Exercise 2

Major Scales, Major Chords & Exercises - G Major

BOTH HANDS

Exercise 3

The Chord

The written symbol for the G Major chord is '**G**Maj'.

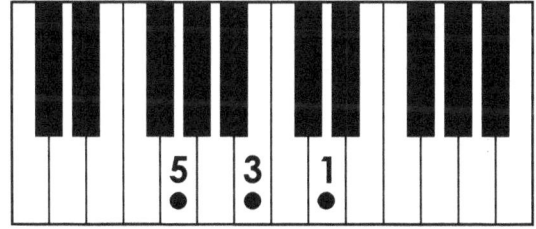

The Left Hand holding **G Major** chord with numbers 5, 3 and 1 fingers.

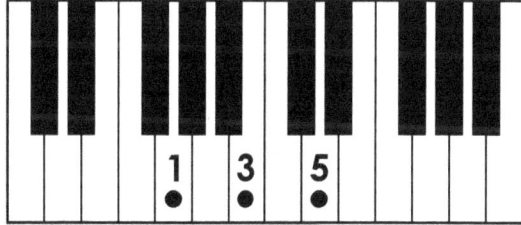

The Right Hand holding **G Major** chord with numbers 1, 3 and 5 fingers.

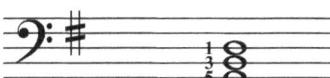

The **G Major** chord written on the Stave (Bass Clef).

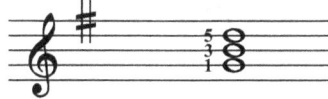

The **G Major** chord written on the Stave (Treble Clef).

Major chords can be played in three different positions. These positions are called Inversions. It is not always possible to hold an inverted chord with numbers 1, 3 and 5 fingers, numbers 2 or 4 fingers may be substituted as needed.

Major Scales, Major Chords & Exercises - G Major

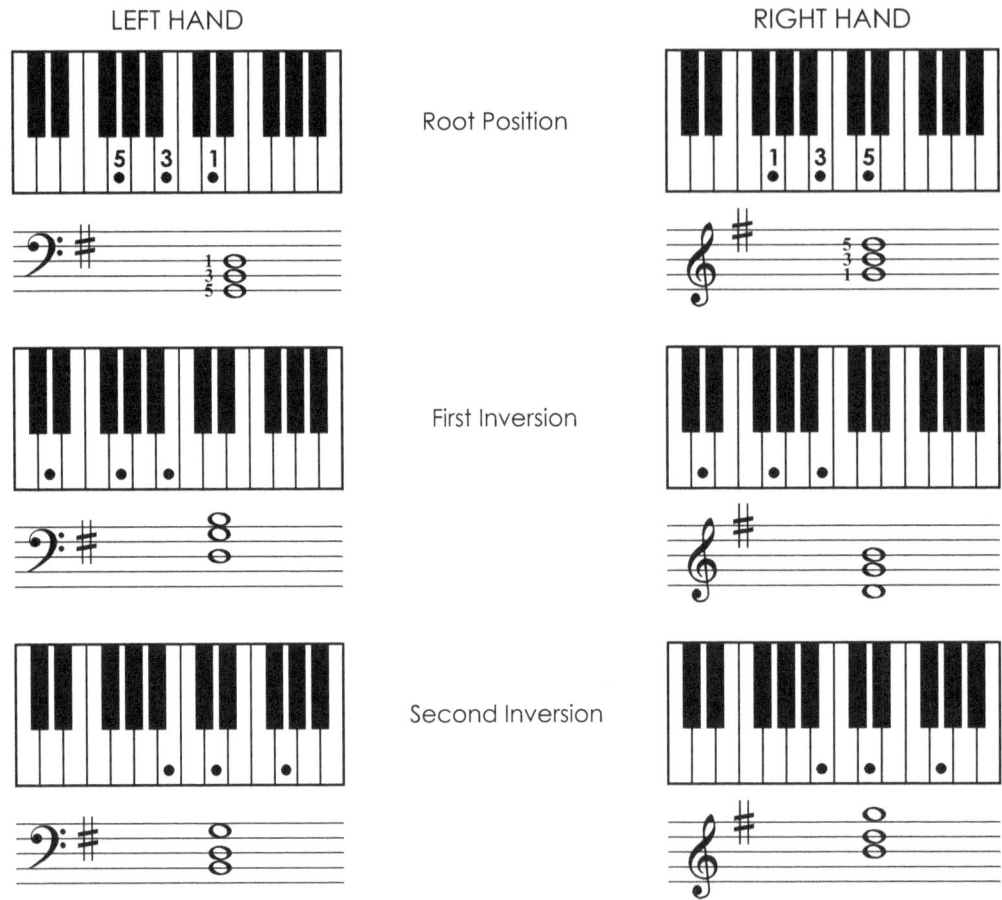

The two pictures below give examples of using both hands to play a chord. The two hand method produces a full or rich sound. Another purpose for the two hand method is to allow the hands to function in separate capacities. For example, the right hand can hold a chord while the left hand plays a pattern or the left hand can hold a chord while the right hand plays a melody, etc.

BOTH HANDS

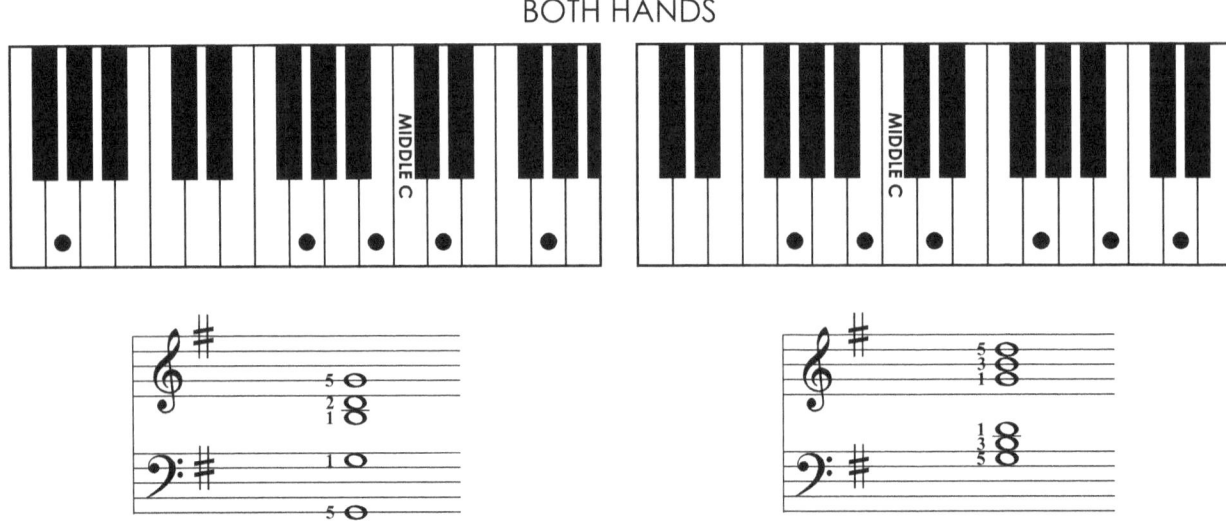

Major Scales, Major Chords & Exercises - G Major

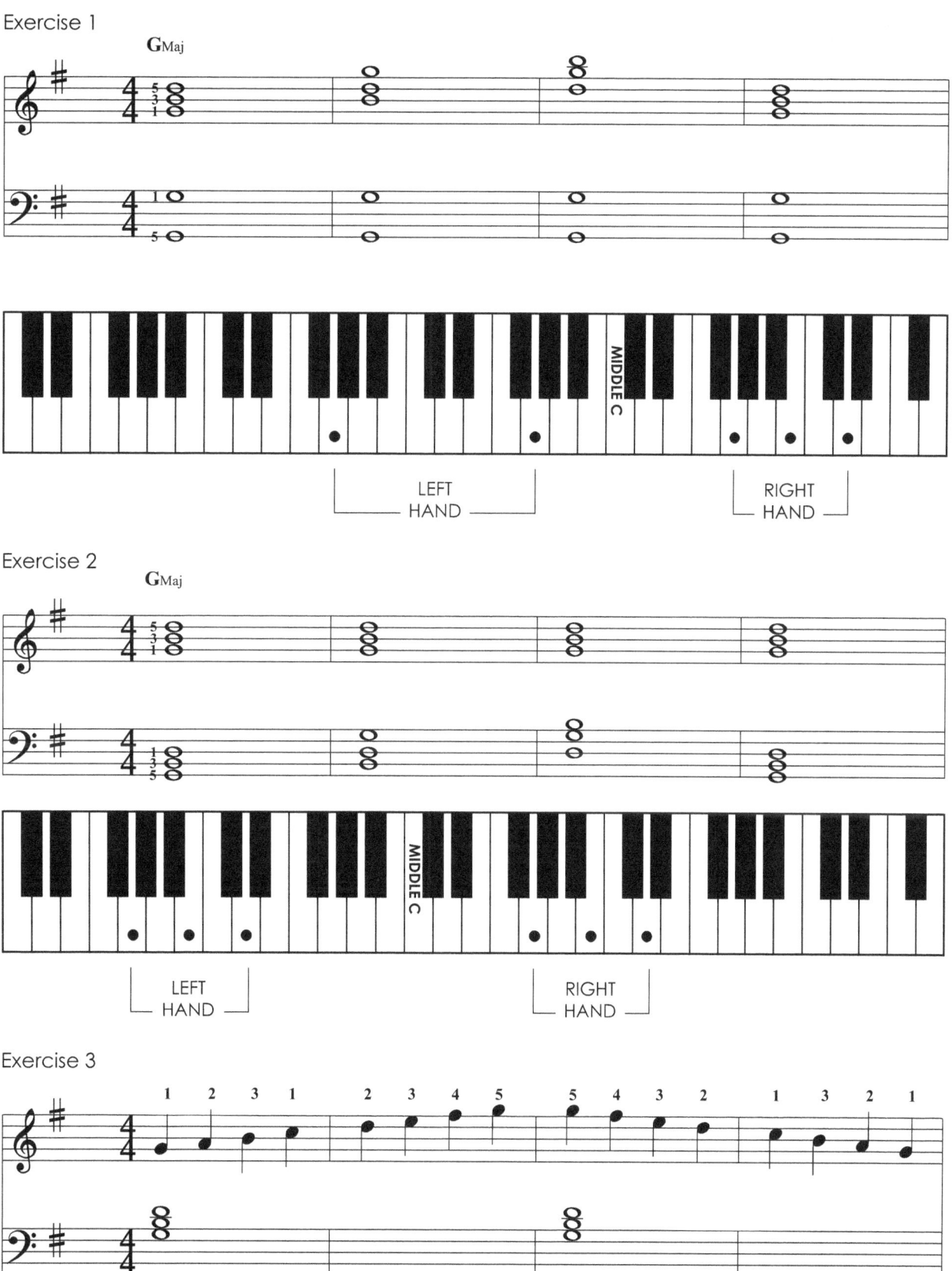

Major Scales, Major Chords & Exercises - *G Major*

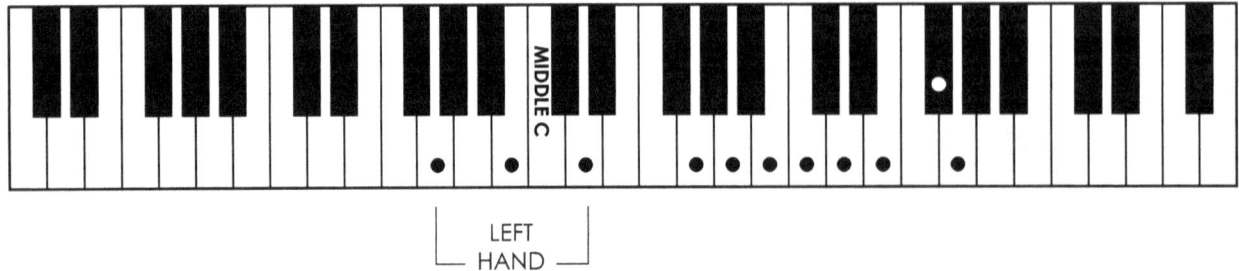

Exercise 4

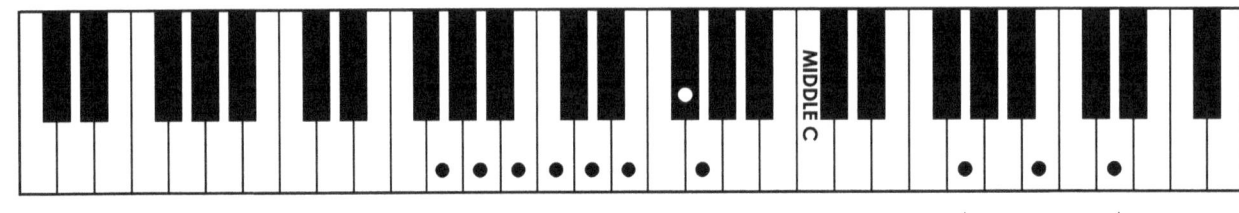

Exercise 5

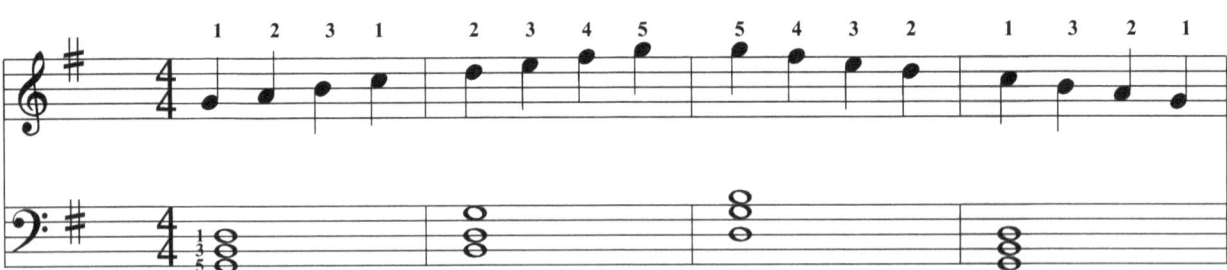

Exercise 6

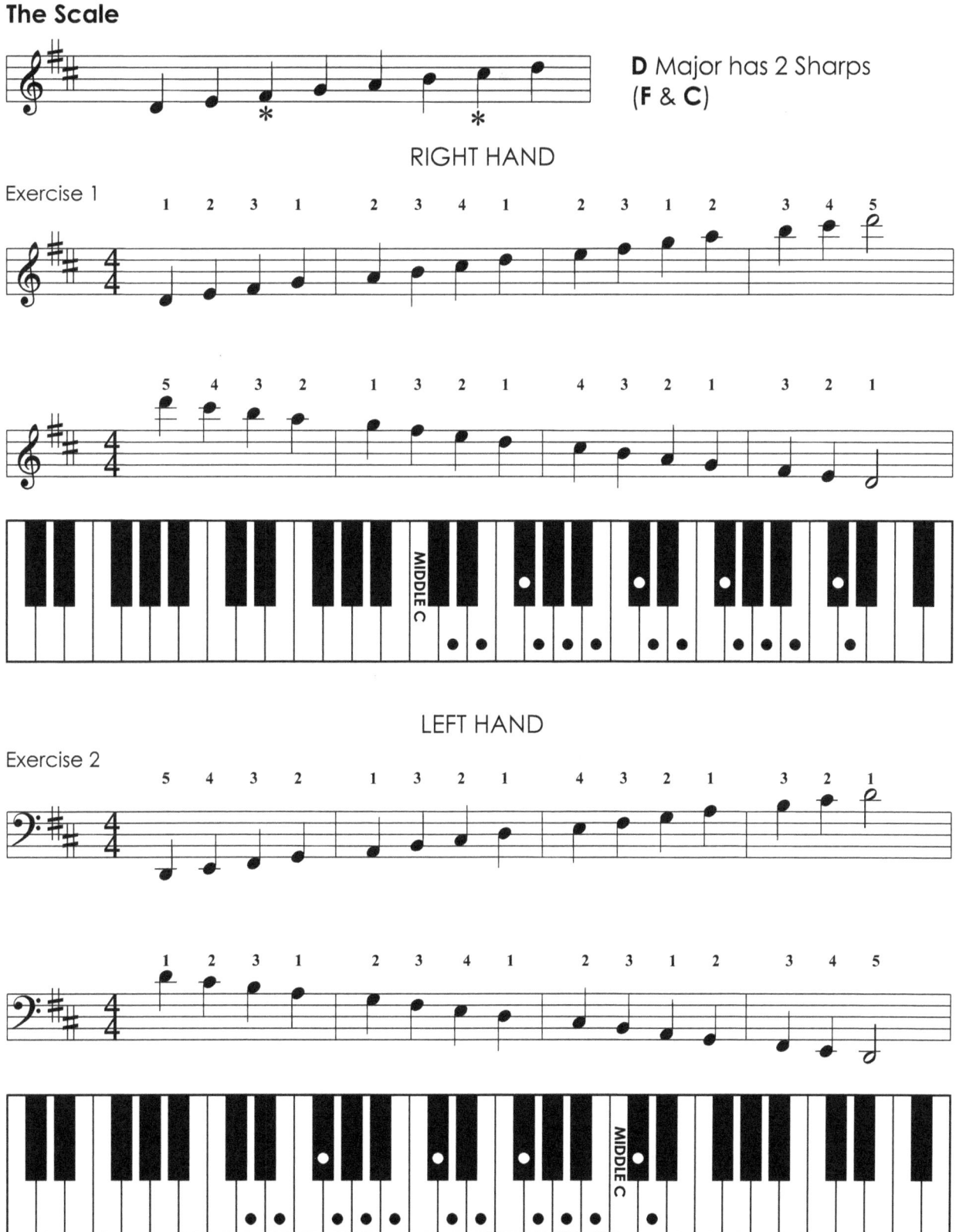

Major Scales, Major Chords & Exercises - *D Major*

BOTH HANDS

Exercise 3

The Chord

The written symbol for the D Major chord is '**D**Maj'.

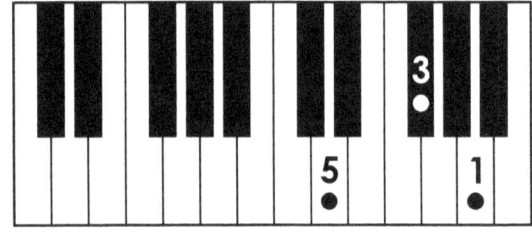

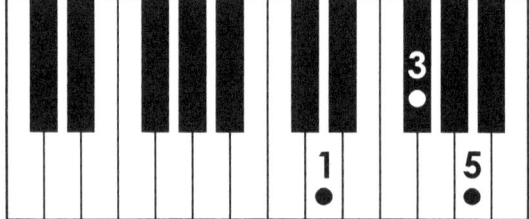

The Left Hand holding **D Major** chord with numbers 5, 3 and 1 fingers.

The Right Hand holding **D Major** chord with numbers 1, 3 and 5 fingers.

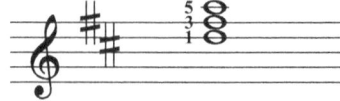

The **D Major** chord written on the Stave (Bass Clef).

The **D Major** chord written on the Stave (Treble Clef).

Major chords can be played in three different positions. These positions are called Inversions. It is not always possible to hold an inverted chord with numbers 1, 3 and 5 fingers, numbers 2 or 4 fingers may be substituted as needed.

Major Scales, Major Chords & Exercises - *D Major*

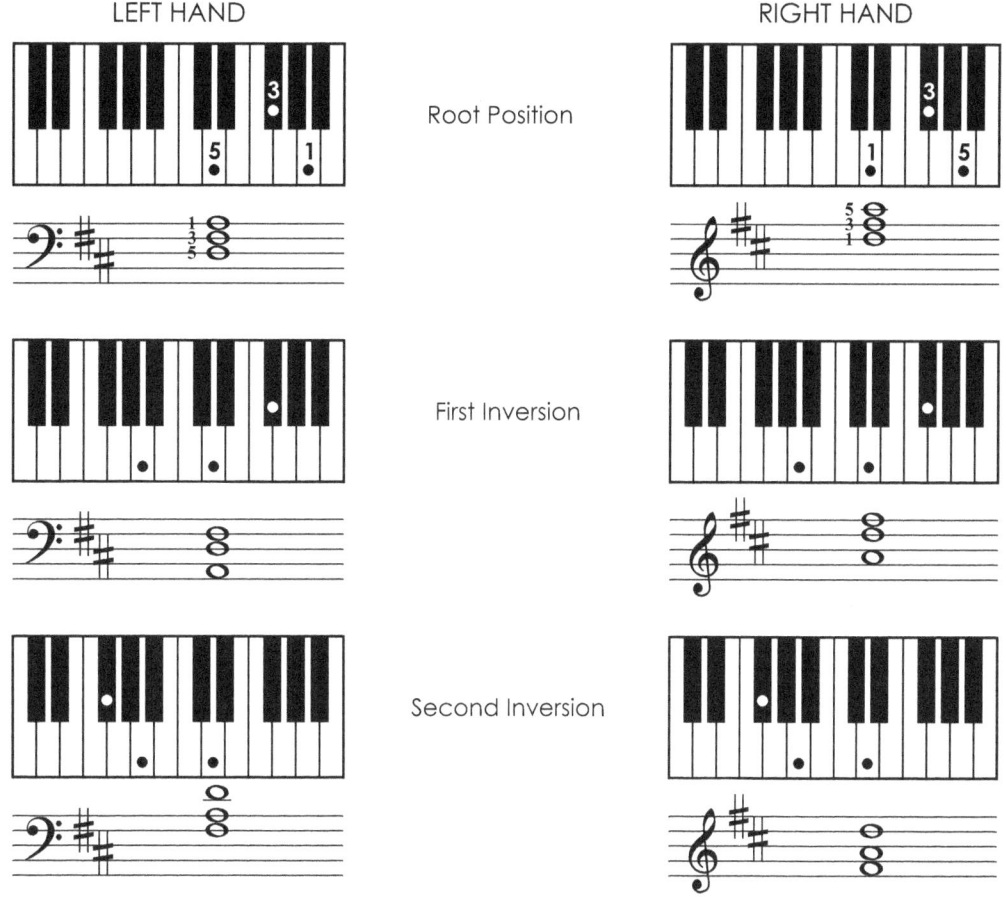

The two pictures below give examples of using both hands to play a chord. The two hand method produces a full or rich sound. Another purpose for the two hand method is to allow the hands to function in separate capacities. For example, the right hand can hold a chord while the left hand plays a pattern or the left hand can hold a chord while the right hand plays a melody, etc.

BOTH HANDS

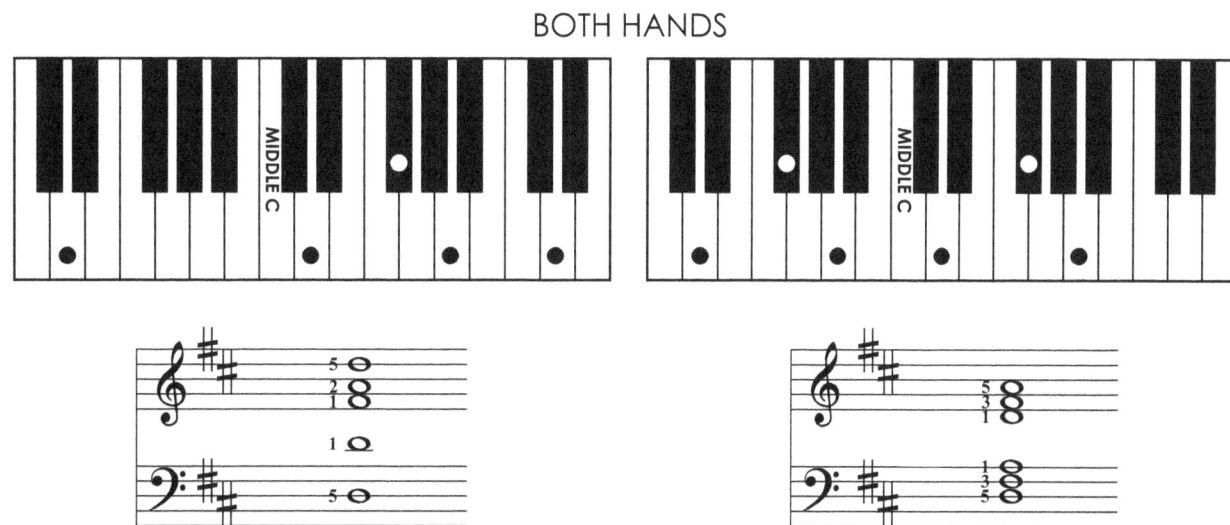

Major Scales, Major Chords & Exercises - *D Major*

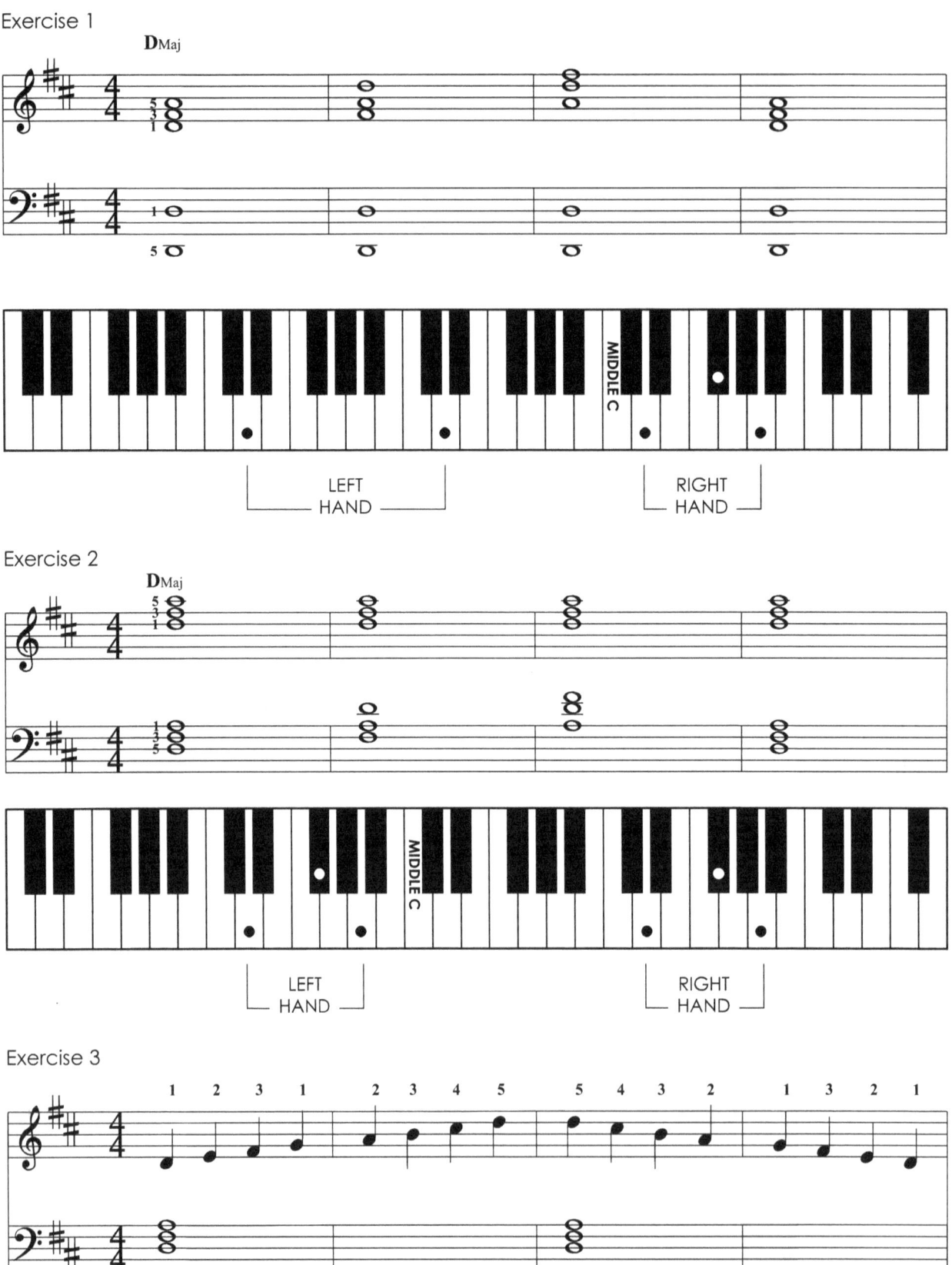

Major Scales, Major Chords & Exercises - *D Major*

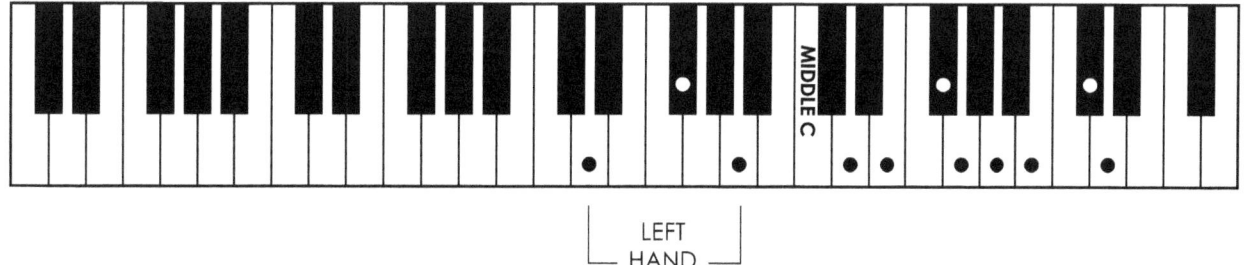

Exercise 4

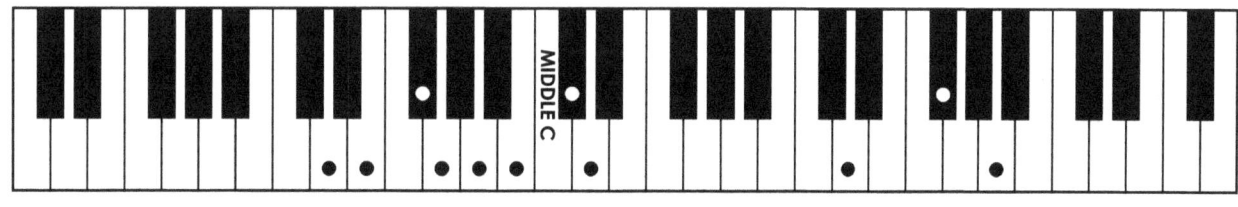

Exercise 5

Exercise 6

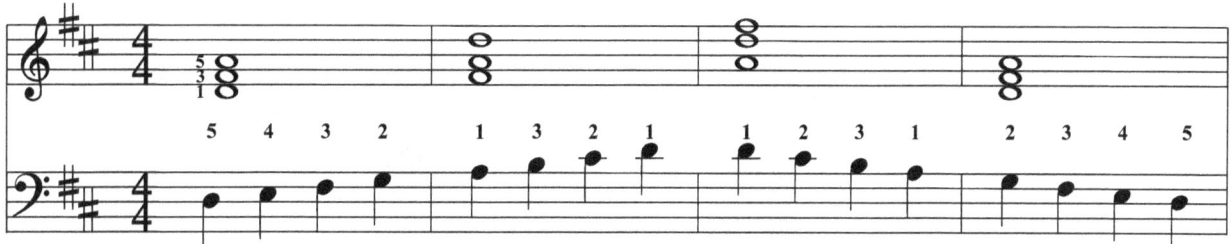

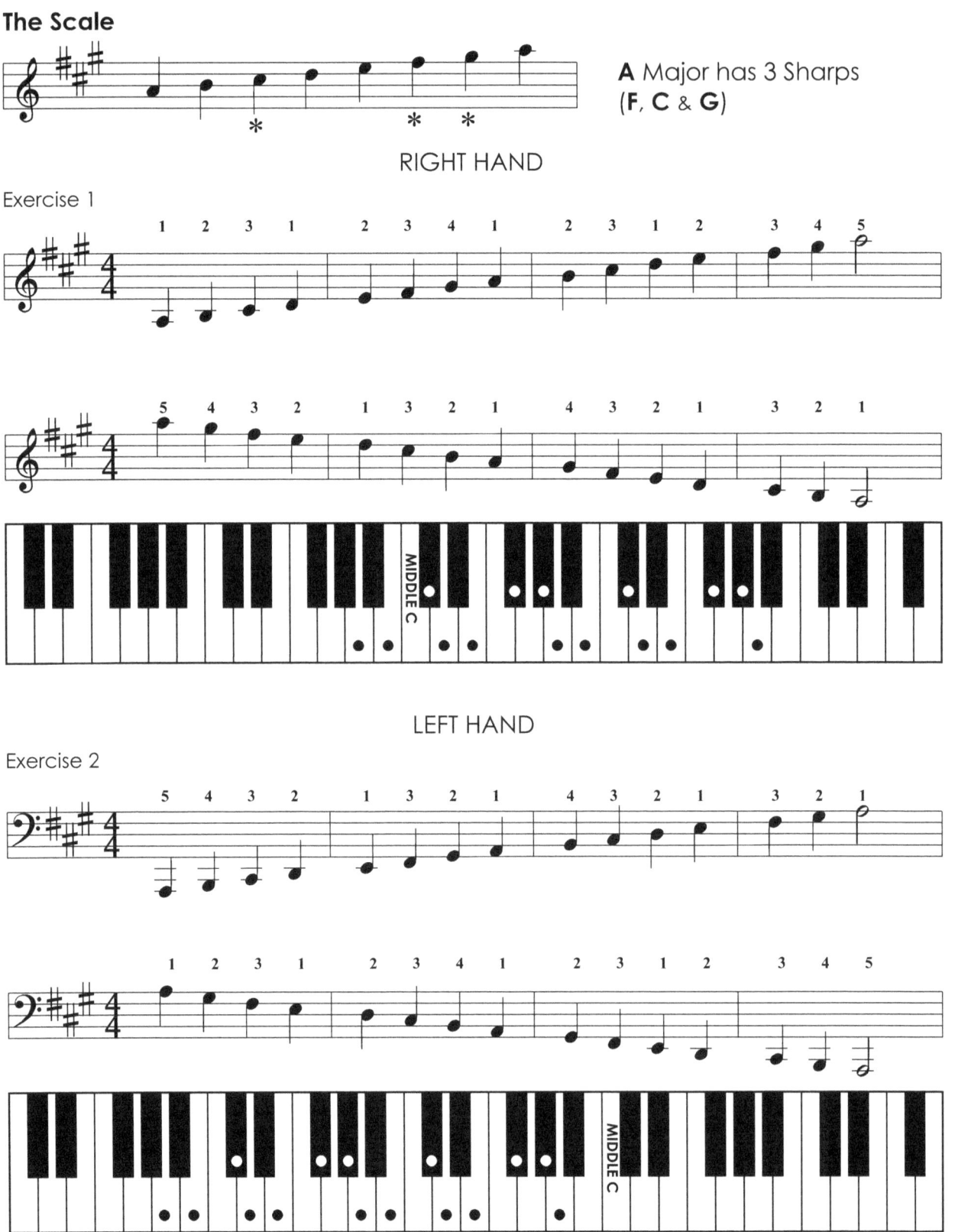

The Key of A Major

34

Major Scales, Major Chords & Exercises - *A Major*

BOTH HANDS

Exercise 3

The Chord

The written symbol for the A Major chord is '**A**Maj'.

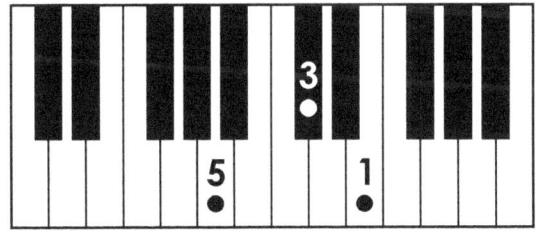

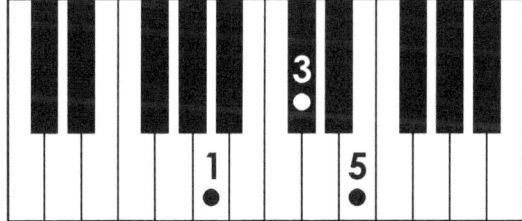

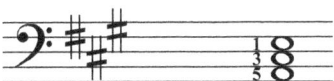

The Left Hand holding **A Major** chord with numbers 5, 3 and 1 fingers.

The Right Hand holding **A Major** chord with numbers 1, 3 and 5 fingers.

The **A Major** chord written on the Stave (Bass Clef).

The **A Major** chord written on the Stave (Treble Clef).

Major chords can be played in three different positions. These positions are called Inversions. It is not always possible to hold an inverted chord with numbers 1, 3 and 5 fingers, numbers 2 or 4 fingers may be substituted as needed.

Major Scales, Major Chords & Exercises - A Major

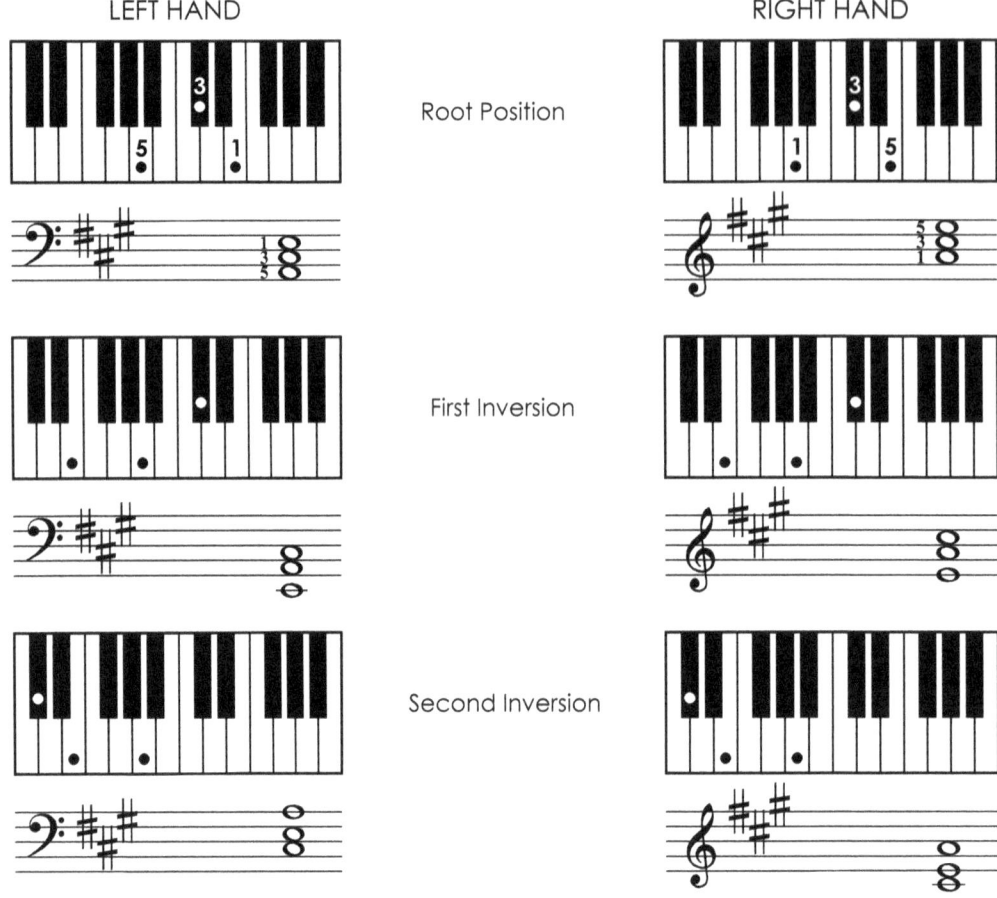

The two pictures below give examples of using both hands to play a chord. The two hand method produces a full or rich sound. Another purpose for the two hand method is to allow the hands to function in separate capacities. For example, the right hand can hold a chord while the left hand plays a pattern or the left hand can hold a chord while the right hand plays a melody, etc.

BOTH HANDS

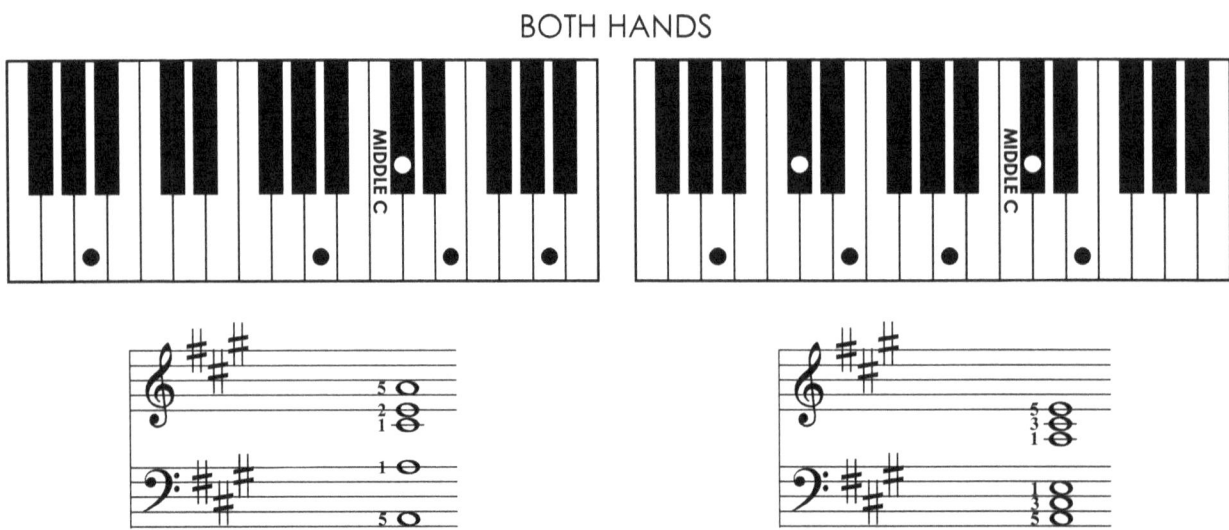

Major Scales, Major Chords & Exercises - A Major

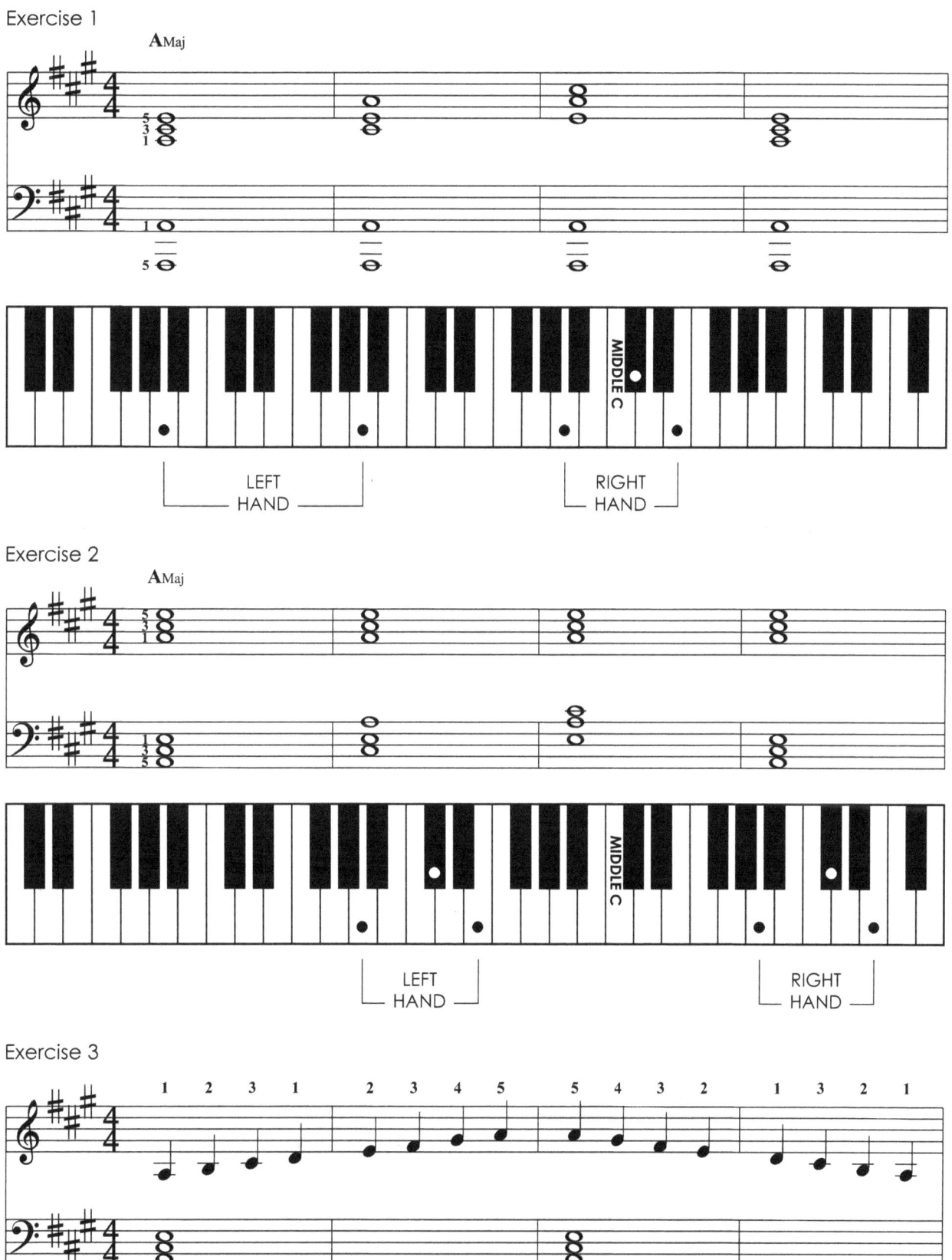

Major Scales, Major Chords & Exercises - *A Major*

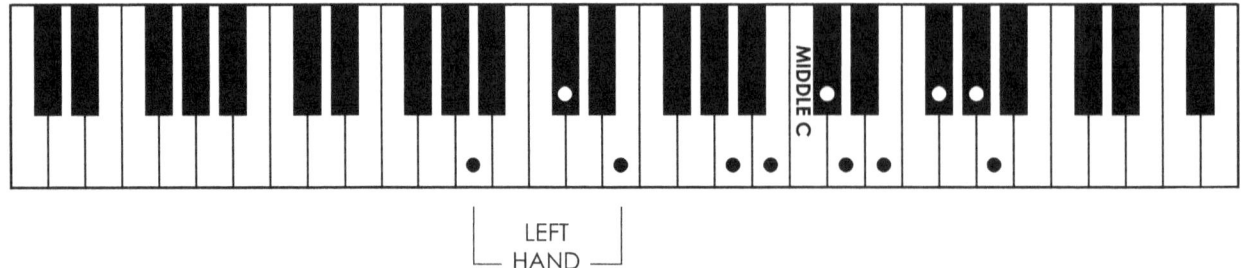

Exercise 4

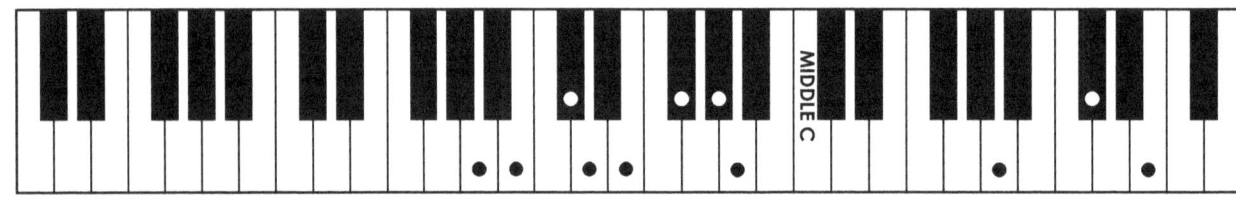

Exercise 5

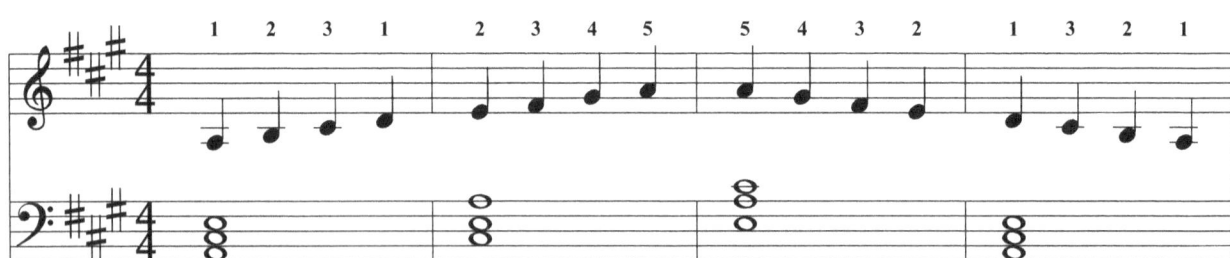

Exercise 6

38

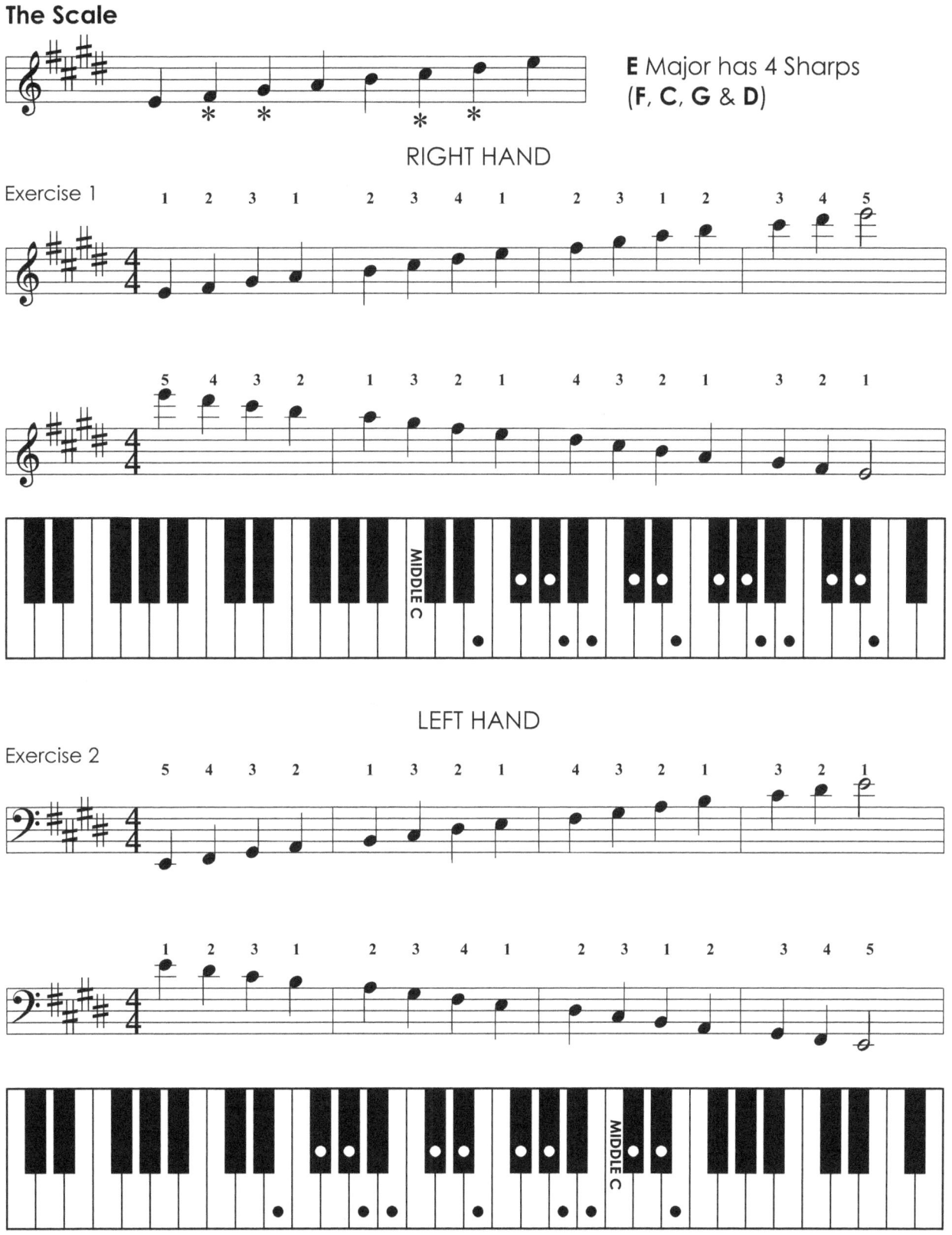

Major Scales, Major Chords & Exercises - *E Major*

BOTH HANDS

Exercise 3

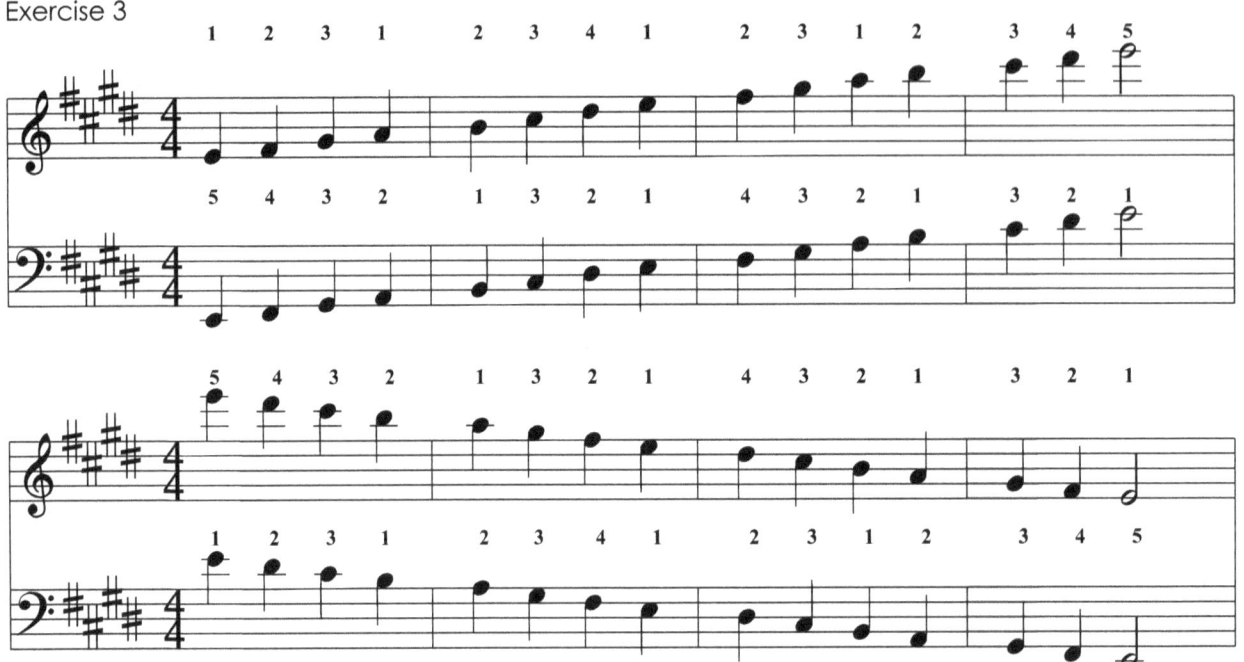

The Chord

The written symbol for the E Major chord is '**E**Maj'.

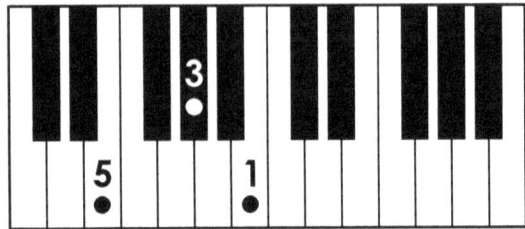

The Left Hand holding **E Major** chord with numbers 5, 3 and 1 fingers.

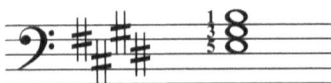

The **E Major** chord written on the Stave (Bass Clef).

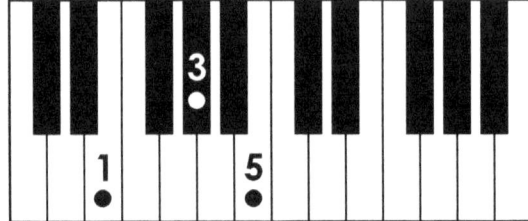

The Right Hand holding **E Major** chord with numbers 1, 3 and 5 fingers.

The **E Major** chord written on the Stave (Treble Clef).

Major chords can be played in three different positions. These positions are called Inversions. It is not always possible to hold an inverted chord with numbers 1, 3 and 5 fingers, numbers 2 or 4 fingers may be substituted as needed.

Major Scales, Major Chords & Exercises - *E Major*

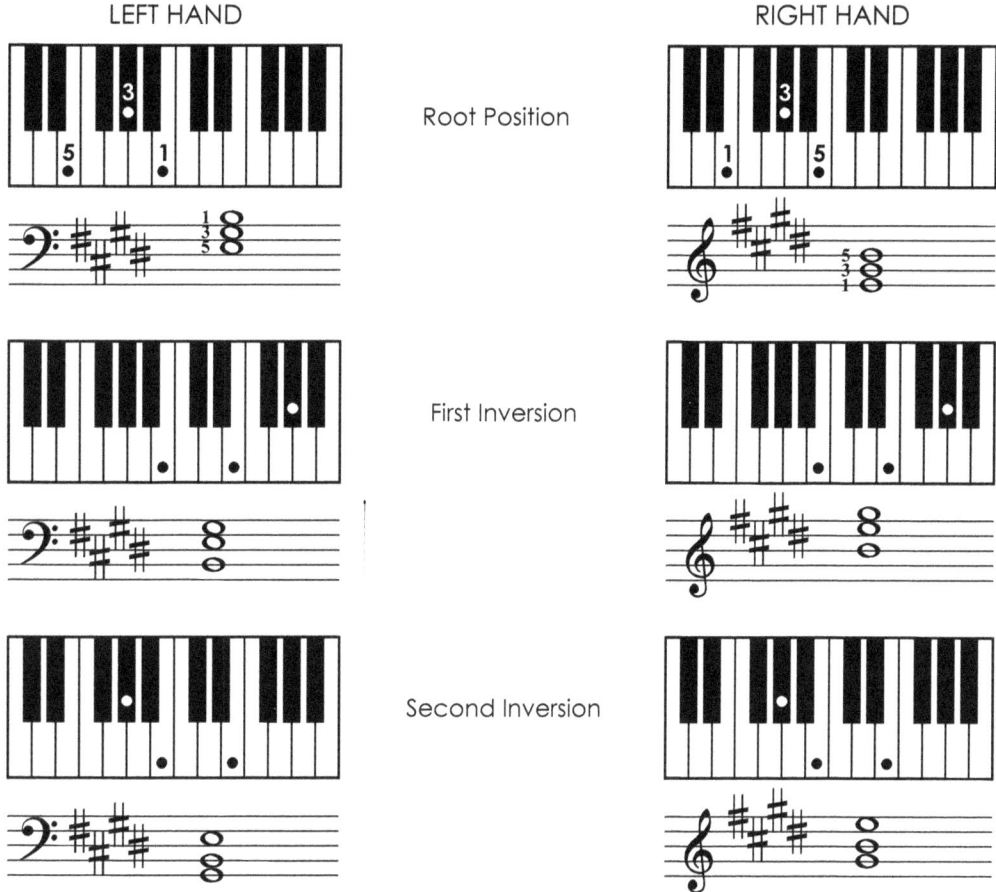

LEFT HAND   RIGHT HAND

Root Position

First Inversion

Second Inversion

The two pictures below give examples of using both hands to play a chord. The two hand method produces a full or rich sound. Another purpose for the two hand method is to allow the hands to function in separate capacities. For example, the right hand can hold a chord while the left hand plays a pattern or the left hand can hold a chord while the right hand plays a melody, etc.

BOTH HANDS

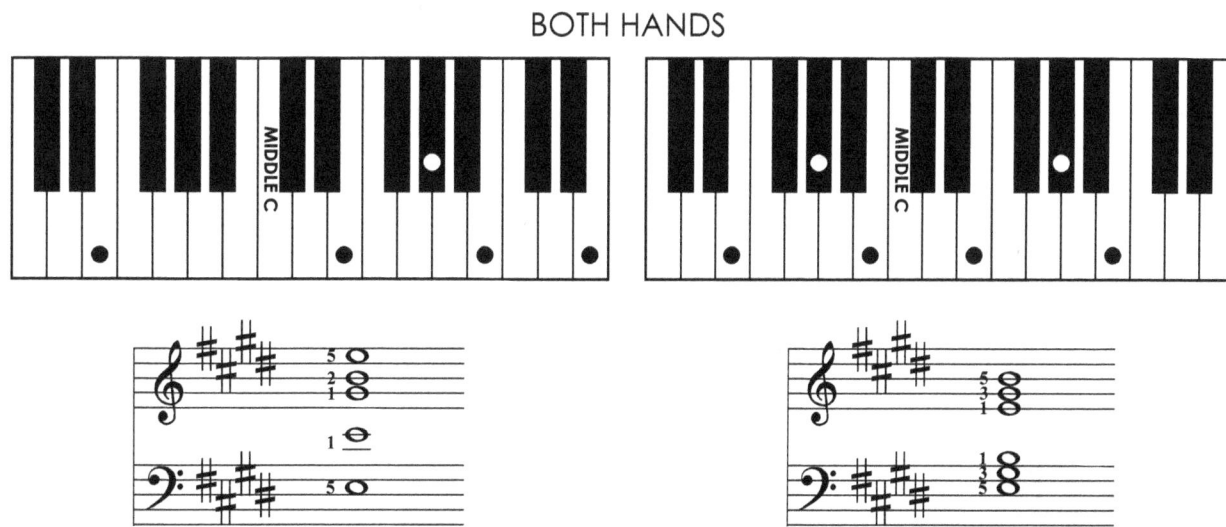

41

Major Scales, Major Chords & Exercises - *E Major*

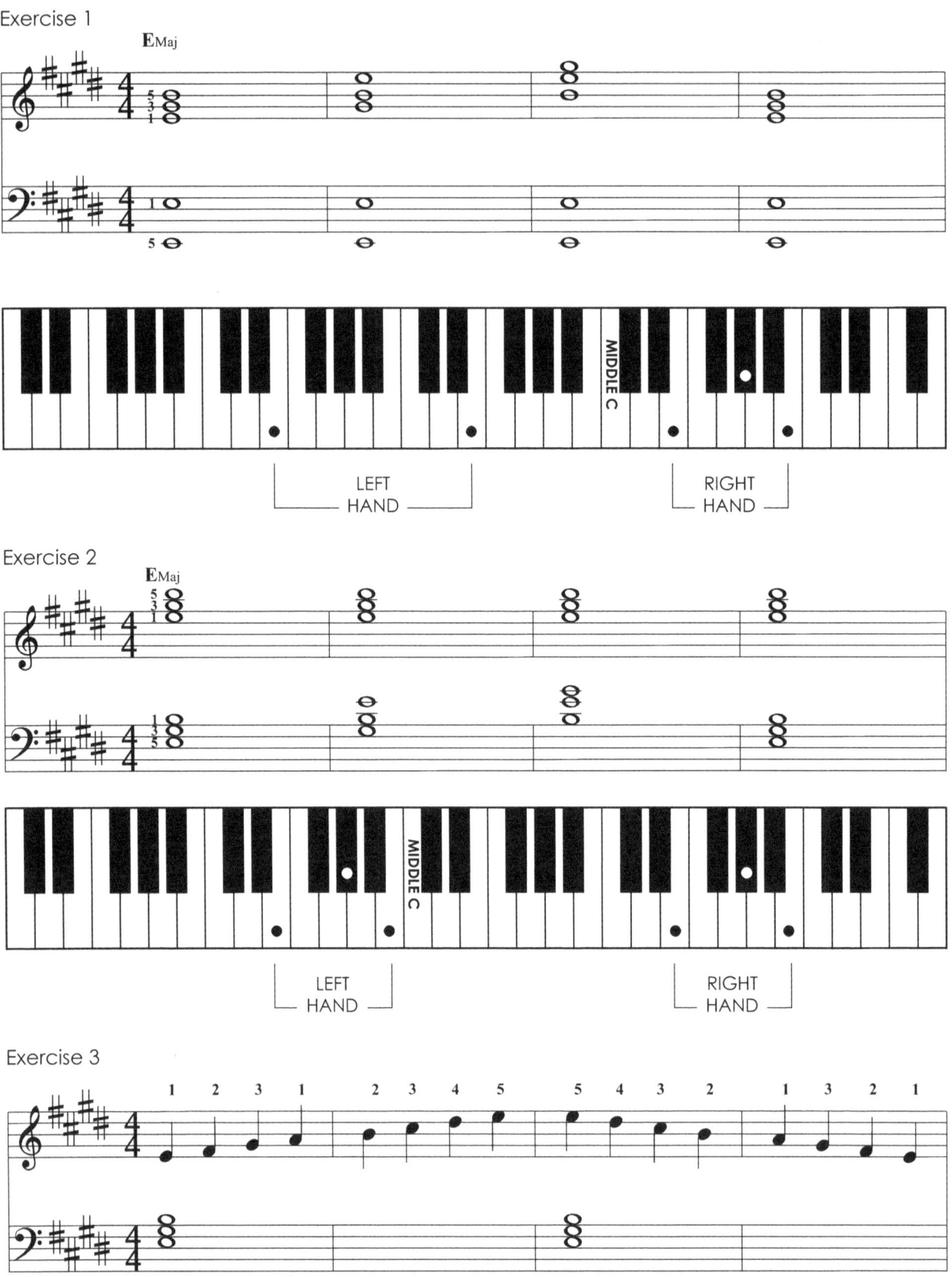

Major Scales, Major Chords & Exercises - *E Major*

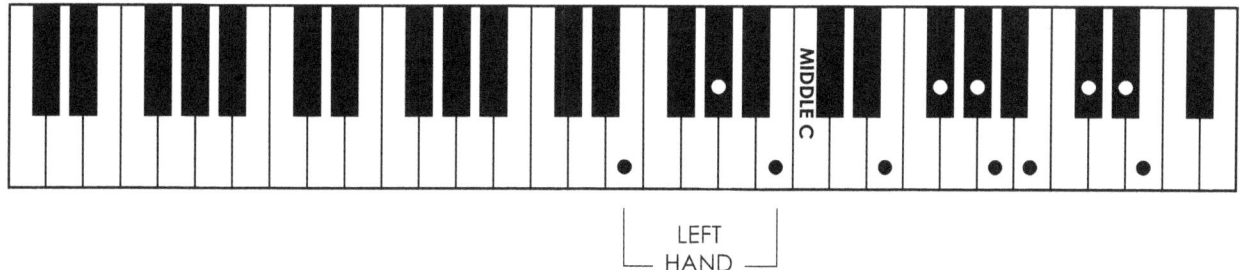

Exercise 4

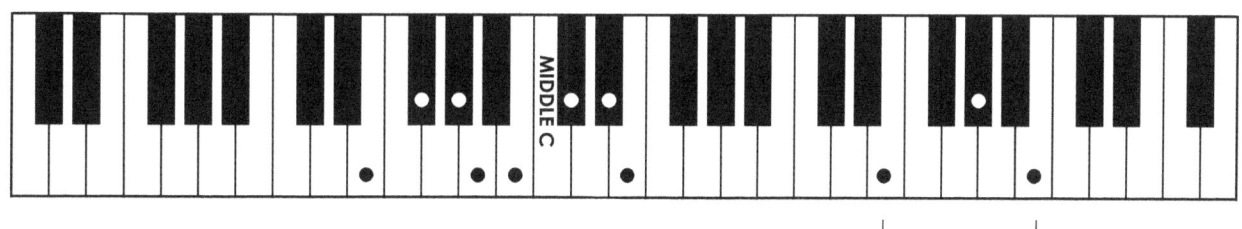

Exercise 5

Exercise 6

43

Major Scales, Major Chords & Exercises - *B Major*

The Key of B Major

The Scale

B Major has 5 Sharps (**F**, **C**, **G**, **D** & **A**)

RIGHT HAND

Exercise 1

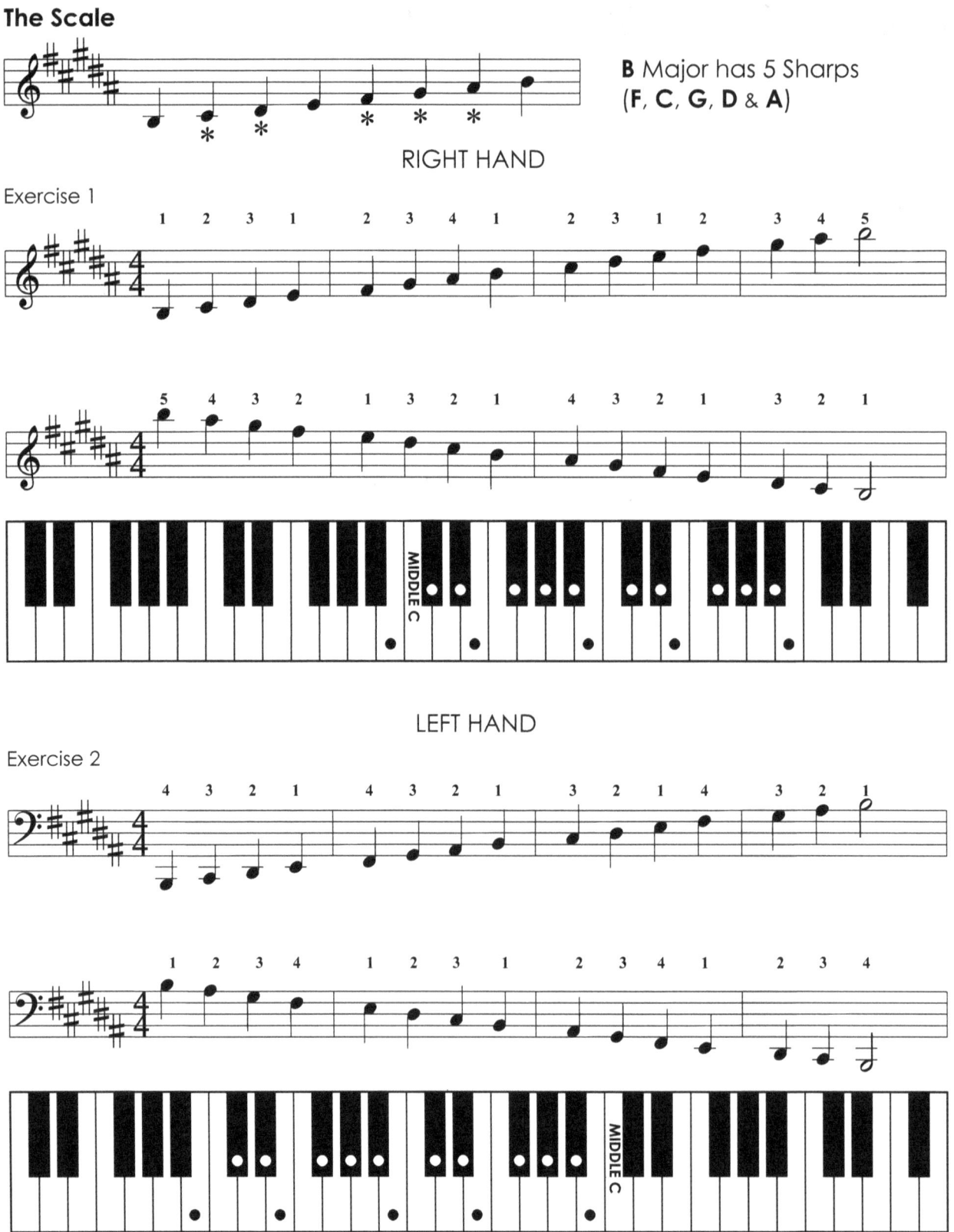

LEFT HAND

Exercise 2

Major Scales, Major Chords & Exercises - *B Major*

BOTH HANDS

Exercise 3

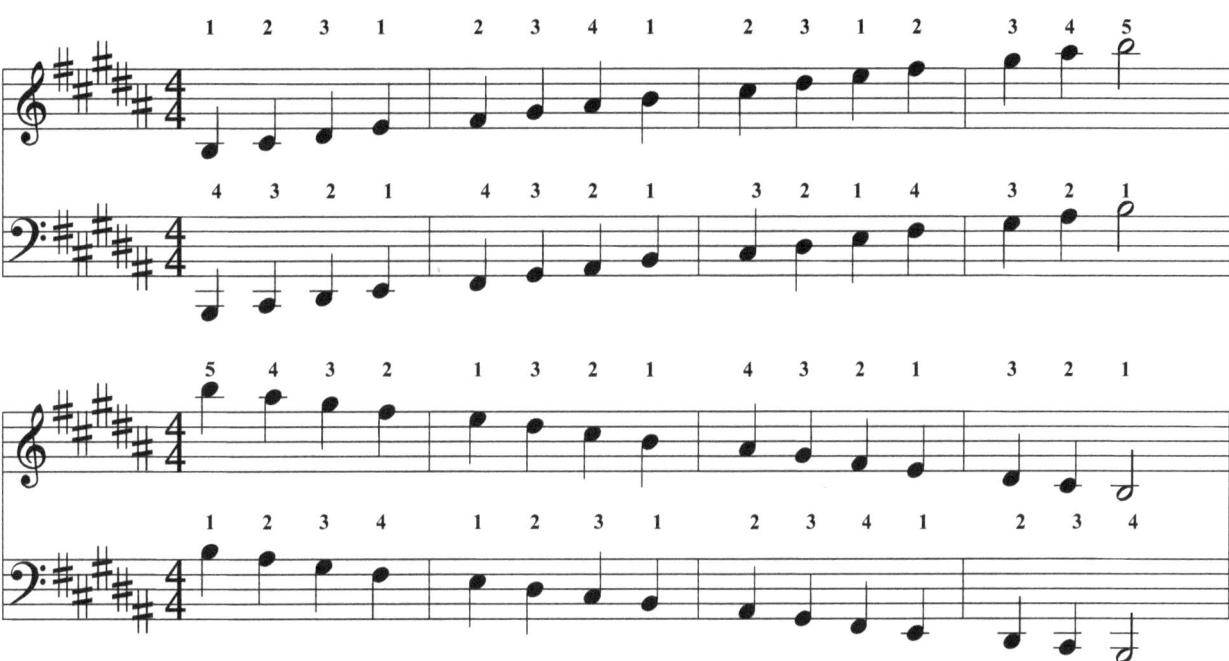

The Chord

The written symbol for the B Major chord is '**B**Maj'.

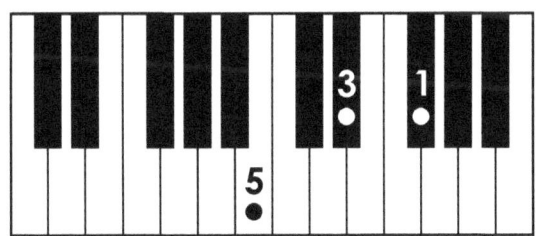

The Left Hand holding **B Major** chord with numbers 5, 3 and 1 fingers.

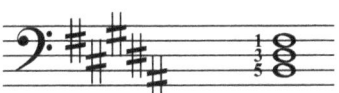

The **B Major** chord written on the Stave (Bass Clef).

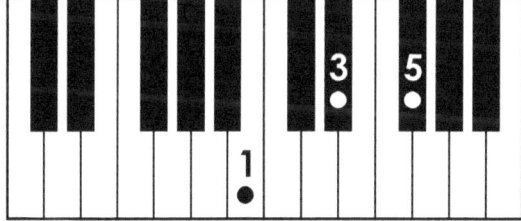

The Right Hand holding **B Major** chord with numbers 1, 3 and 5 fingers.

The **B Major** chord written on the Stave (Treble Clef).

Major chords can be played in three different positions. These positions are called Inversions. It is not always possible to hold an inverted chord with numbers 1, 3 and 5 fingers, numbers 2 or 4 fingers may be substituted as needed.

Major Scales, Major Chords & Exercises - *B Major*

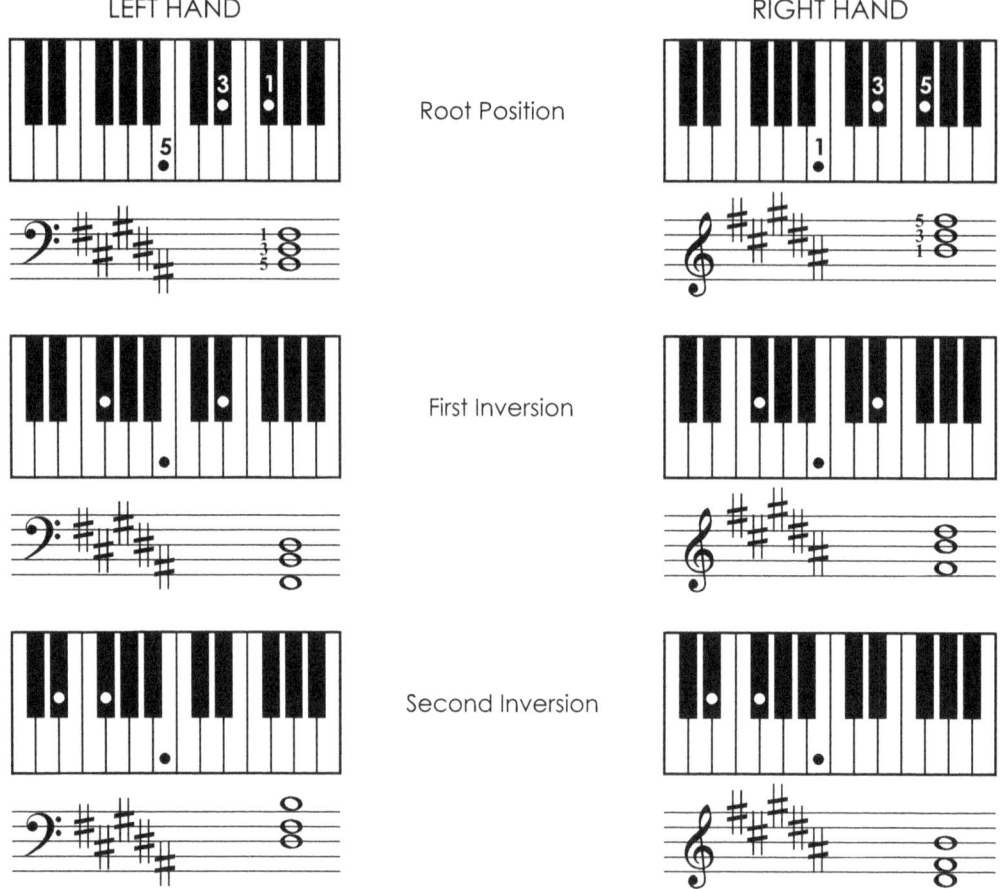

The two pictures below give examples of using both hands to play a chord. The two hand method produces a full or rich sound. Another purpose for the two hand method is to allow the hands to function in separate capacities. For example, the right hand can hold a chord while the left hand plays a pattern or the left hand can hold a chord while the right hand plays a melody, etc.

BOTH HANDS

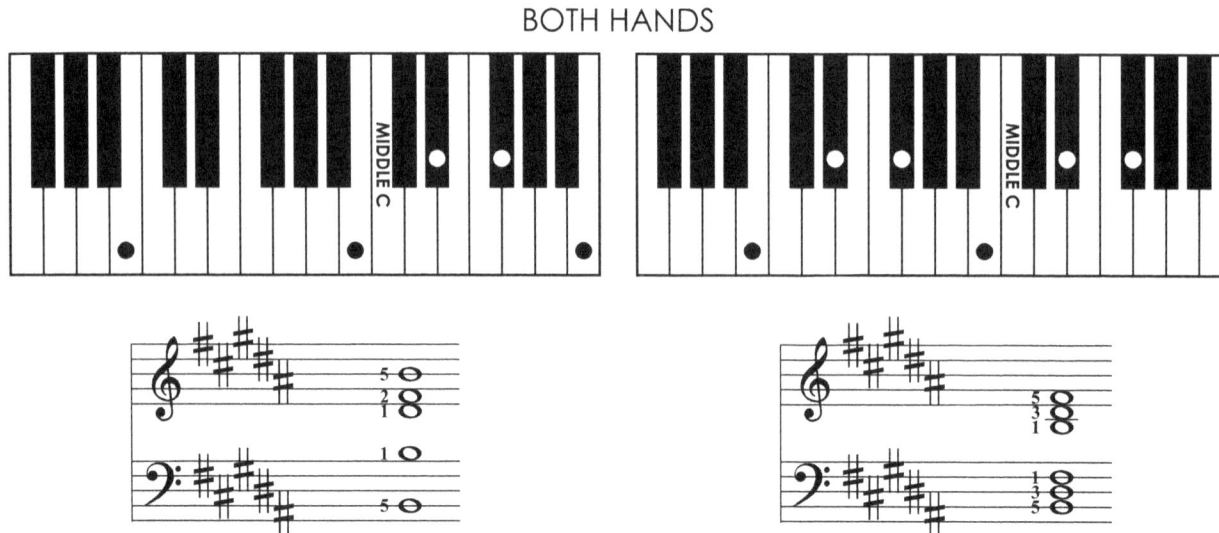

Major Scales, Major Chords & Exercises - *B Major*

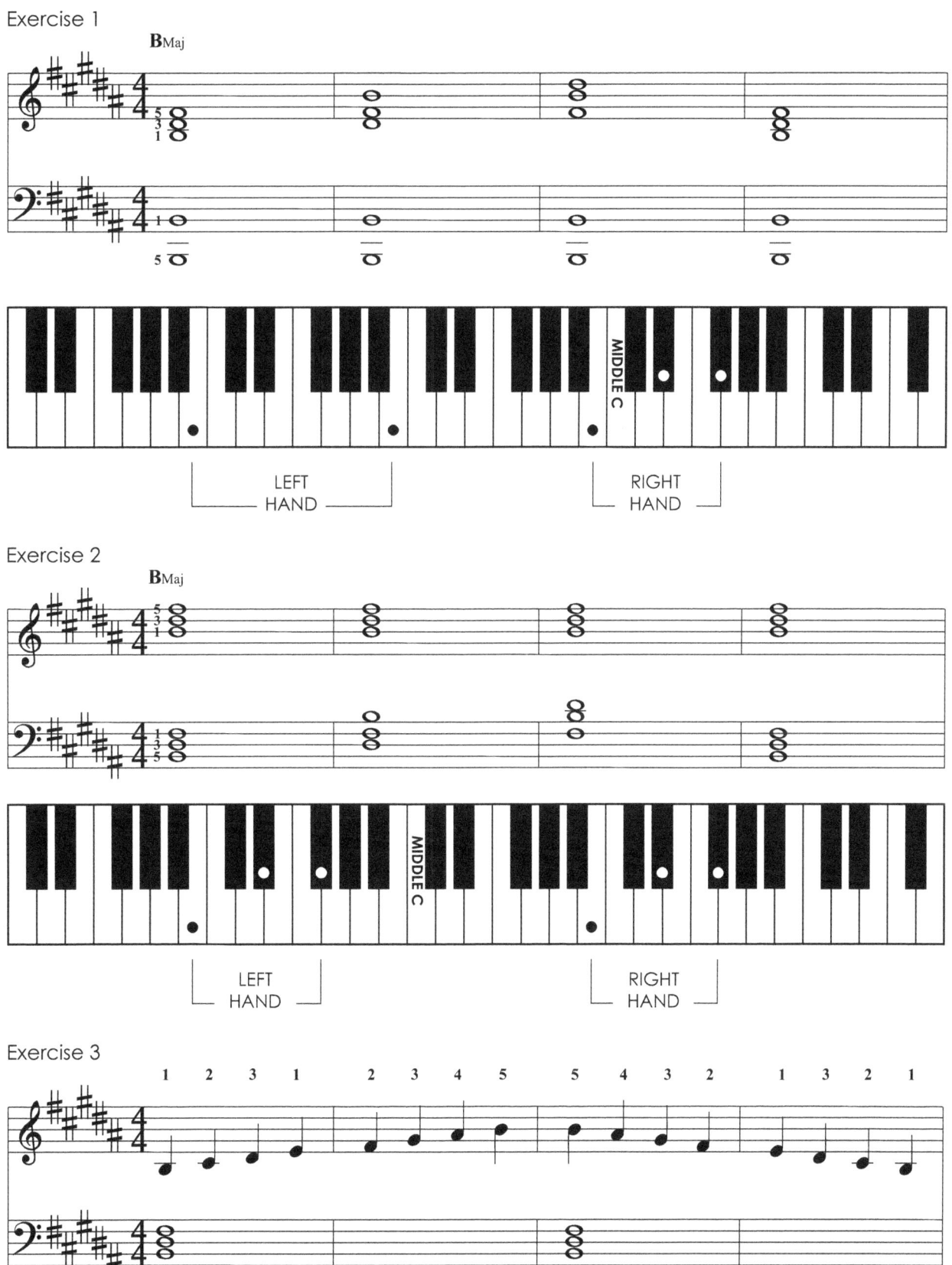

Major Scales, Major Chords & Exercises - *B Major*

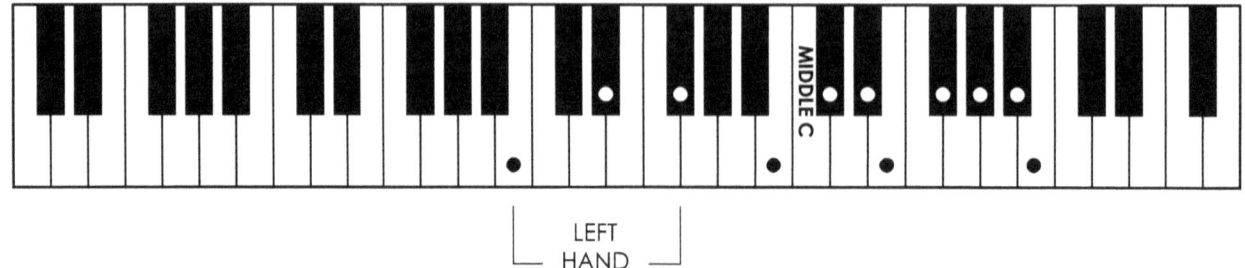

Exercise 4

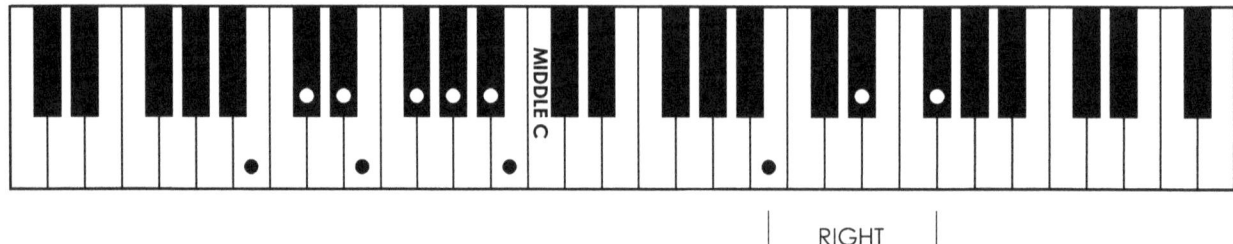

Exercise 5

Exercise 6

48

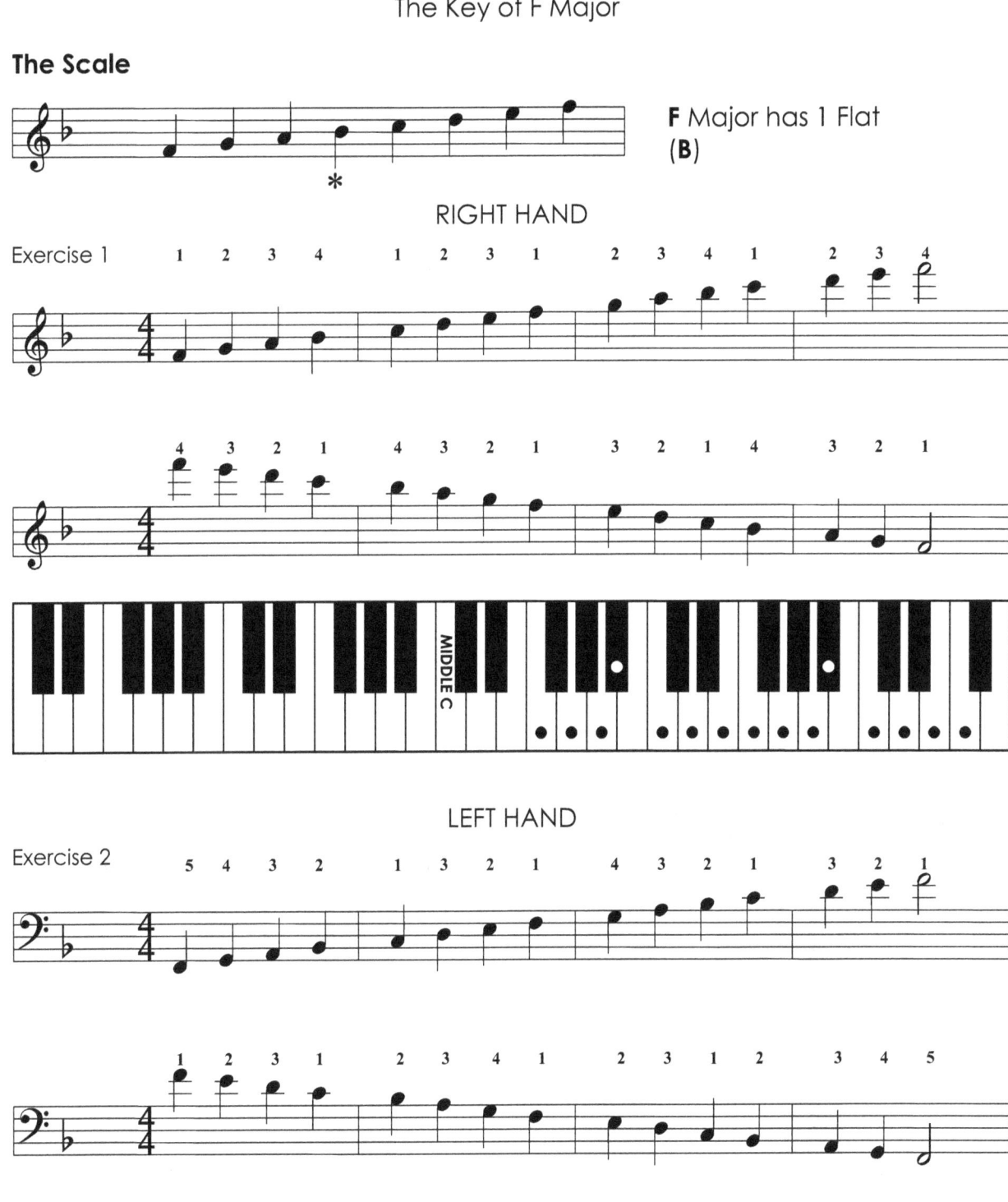

Major Scales, Major Chords & Exercises - *F Major*

BOTH HANDS

Exercise 3

The Chord

The written symbol for the F Major chord is '**F**Maj'.

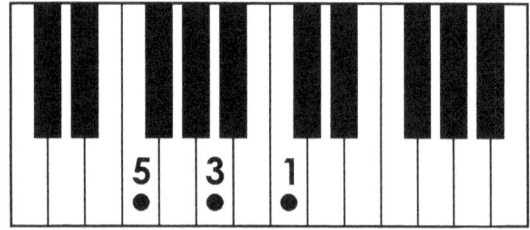

The Left Hand holding **F Major** chord with numbers 5, 3 and 1 fingers.

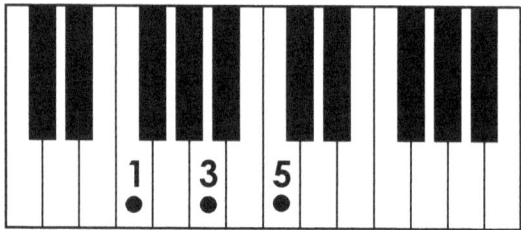

The Right Hand holding **F Major** chord with numbers 1, 3 and 5 fingers.

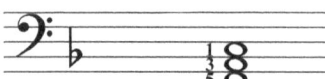

The **F Major** chord written on the Stave (Bass Clef).

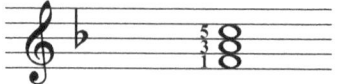

The **F Major** chord written on the Stave (Treble Clef).

Major chords can be played in three different positions. These positions are called Inversions. It is not always possible to hold an inverted chord with numbers 1, 3 and 5 fingers, numbers 2 or 4 fingers may be substituted as needed.

Major Scales, Major Chords & Exercises - *F Major*

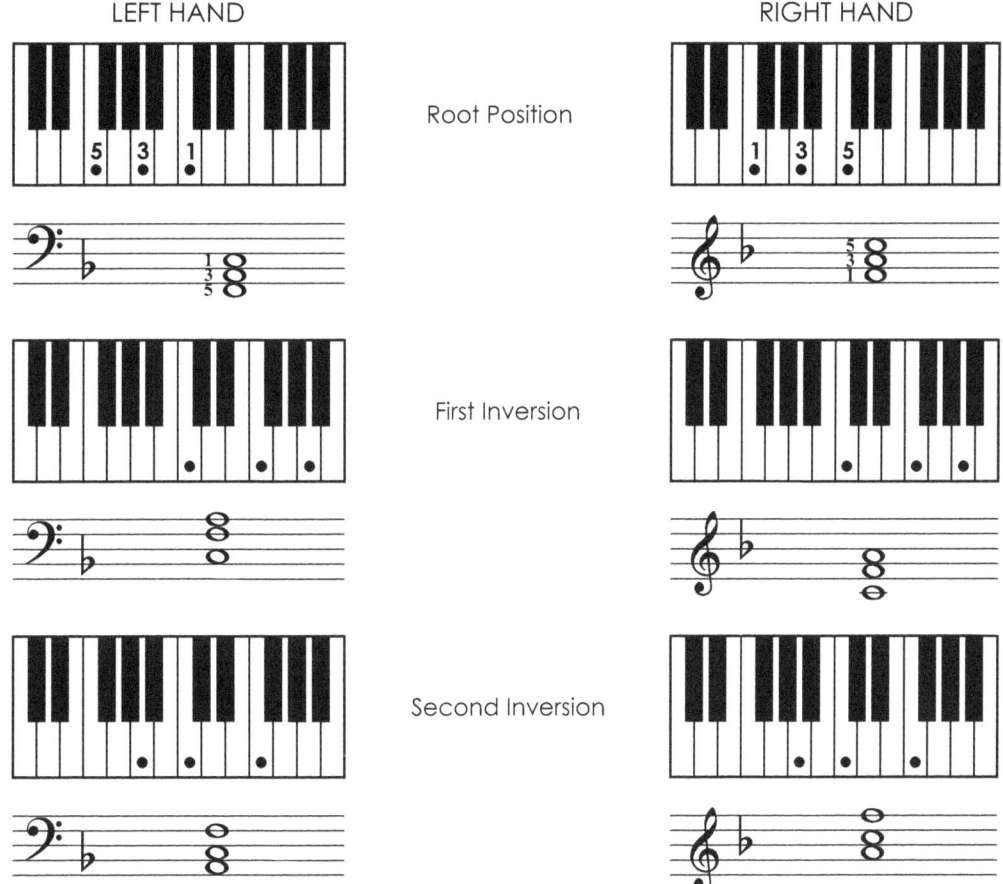

The two pictures below give examples of using both hands to play a chord. The two hand method produces a full or rich sound. Another purpose for the two hand method is to allow the hands to function in separate capacities. For example, the right hand can hold a chord while the left hand plays a pattern or the left hand can hold a chord while the right hand plays a melody, etc.

BOTH HANDS

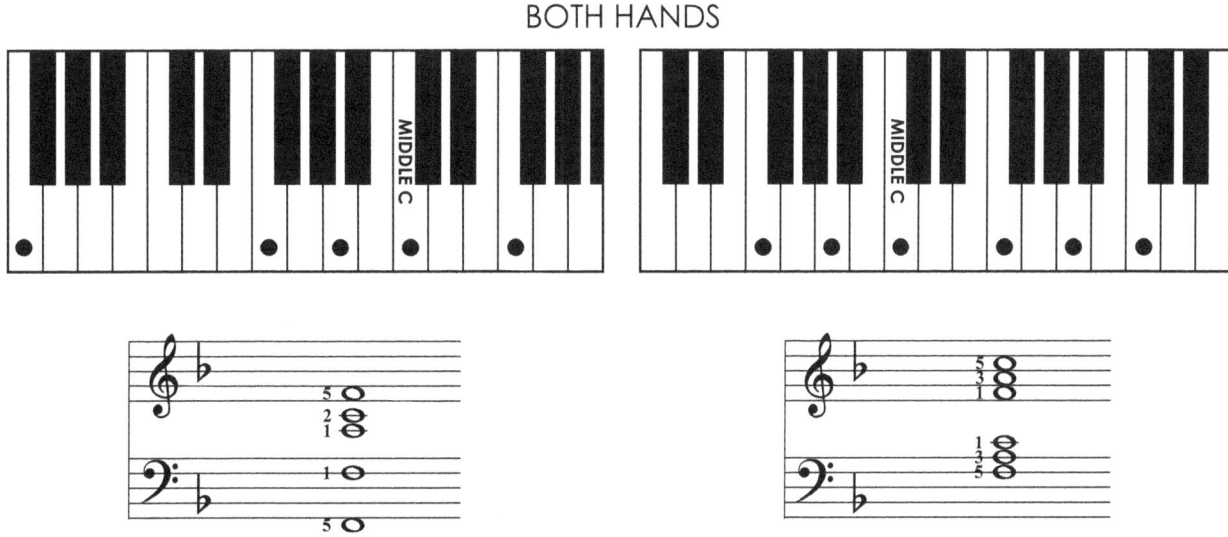

51

Major Scales, Major Chords & Exercises - *F Major*

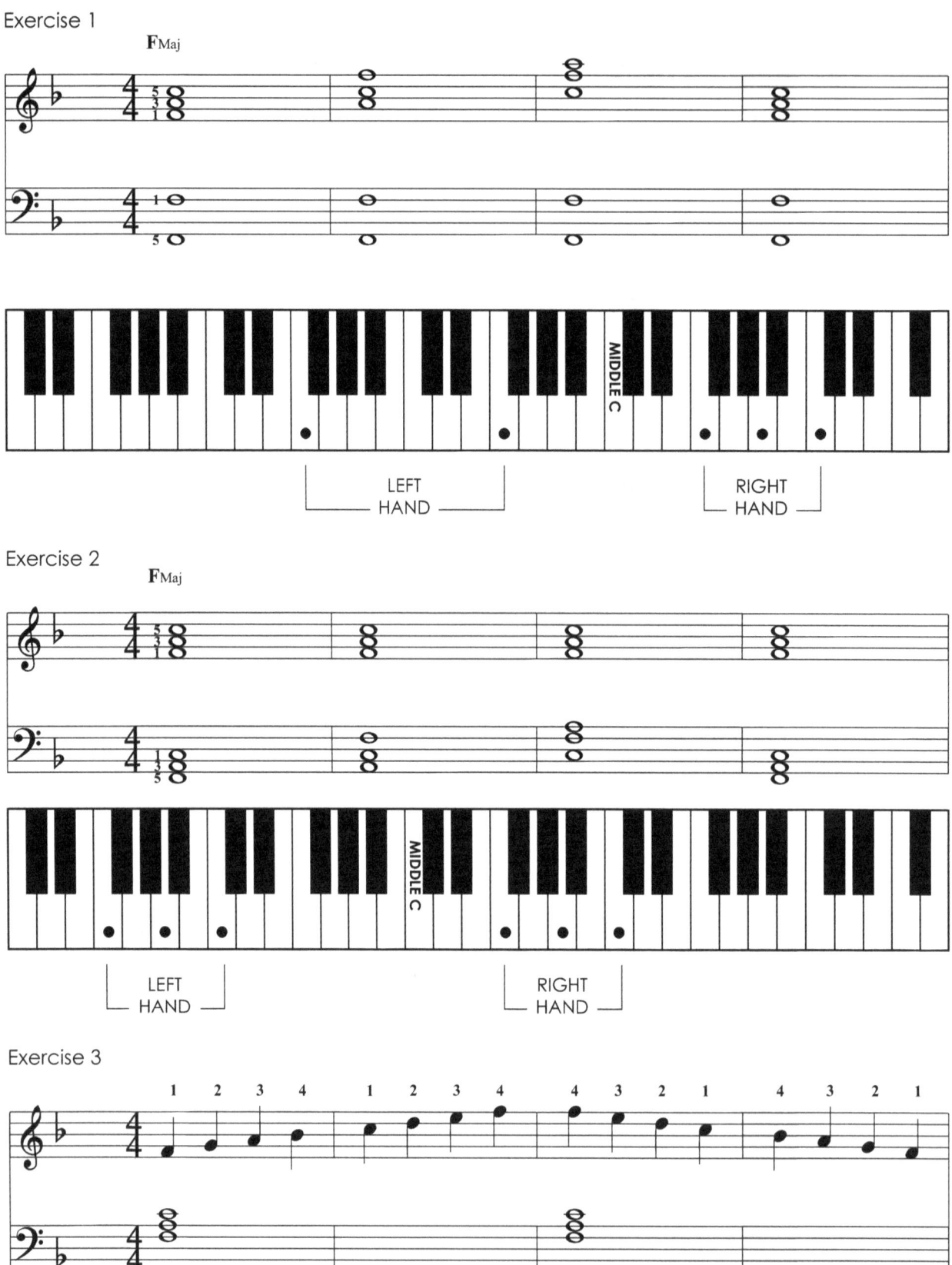

Major Scales, Major Chords & Exercises - *F Major*

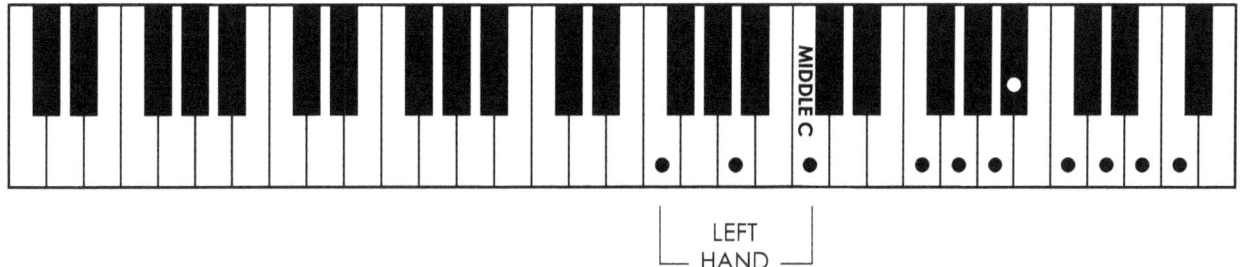

Exercise 4

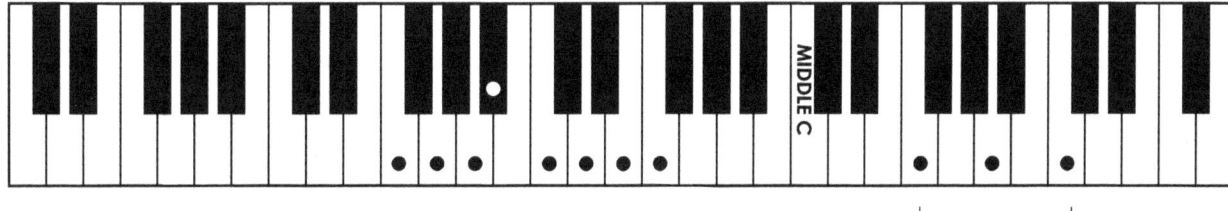

Exercise 5

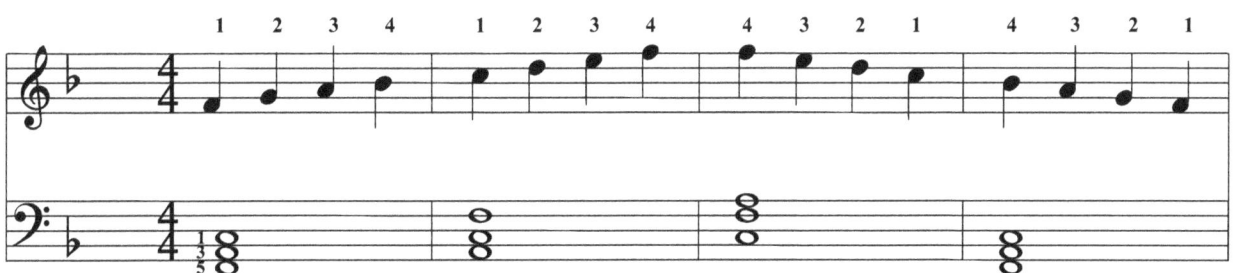

Exercise 6

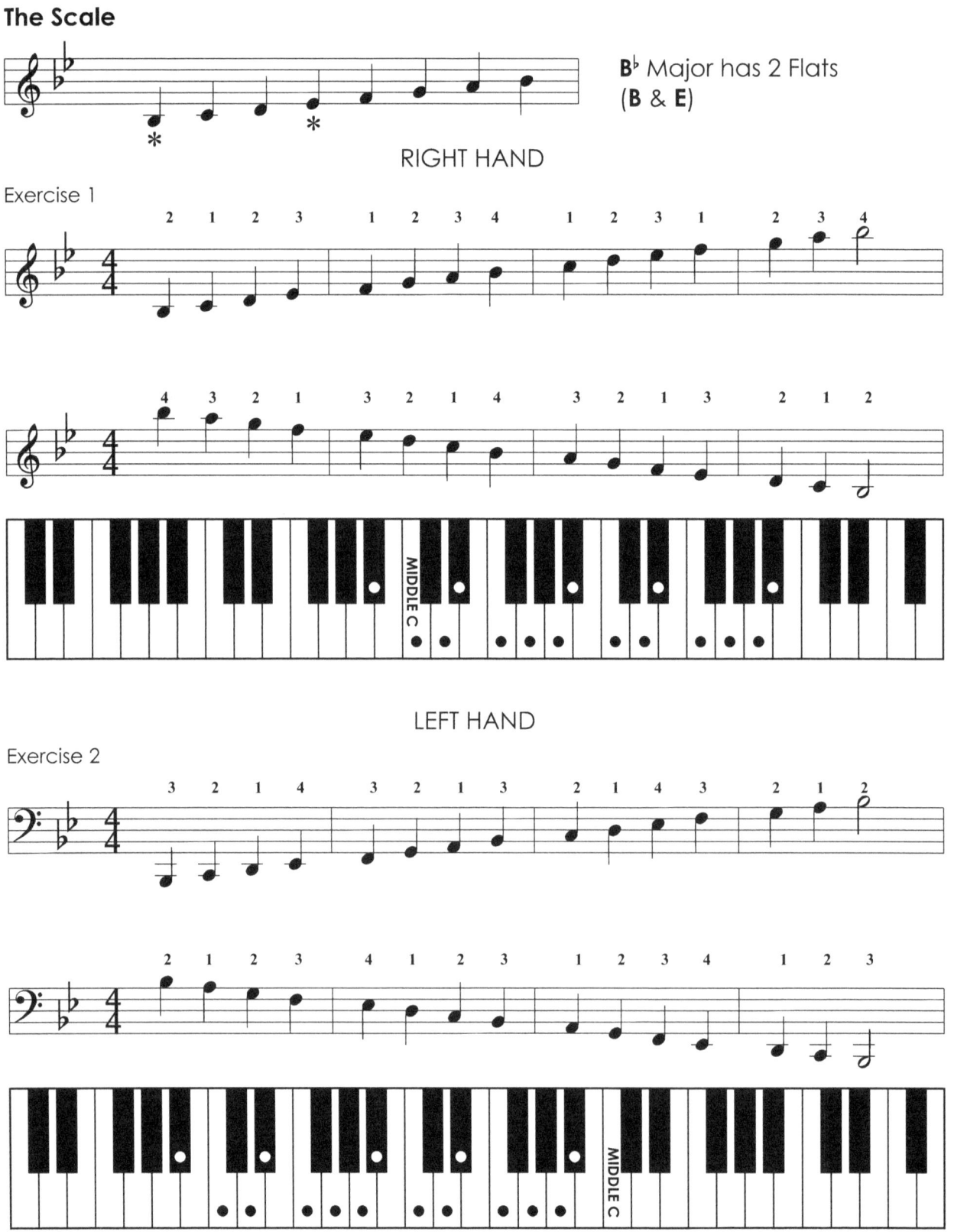

Major Scales, Major Chords & Exercises - B♭ Major

BOTH HANDS

Exercise 3

The Chord

The written symbol for the B♭ Major chord is '**B♭** Maj'.

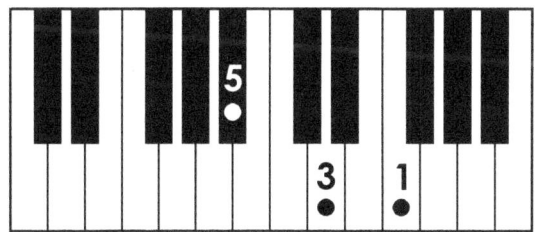

The Left Hand holding **B♭ Major** chord with the number 5, 3 and 1 fingers.

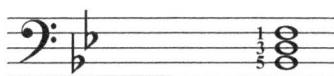

The **B♭ Major** chord written on the Stave (Bass Clef).

The Right Hand holding **B♭ Major** chord with the number 1, 3 and 5 fingers.

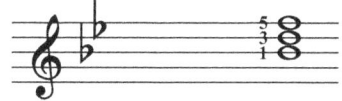

The **B♭ Major** chord written on the Stave (Treble Clef).

Major chords can be played in three different positions. These positions are called Inversions. It is not always possible to hold an inverted chord with numbers 1, 3 and 5 fingers, numbers 2 or 4 fingers may be substituted as needed.

Major Scales, Major Chords & Exercises - B♭ Major

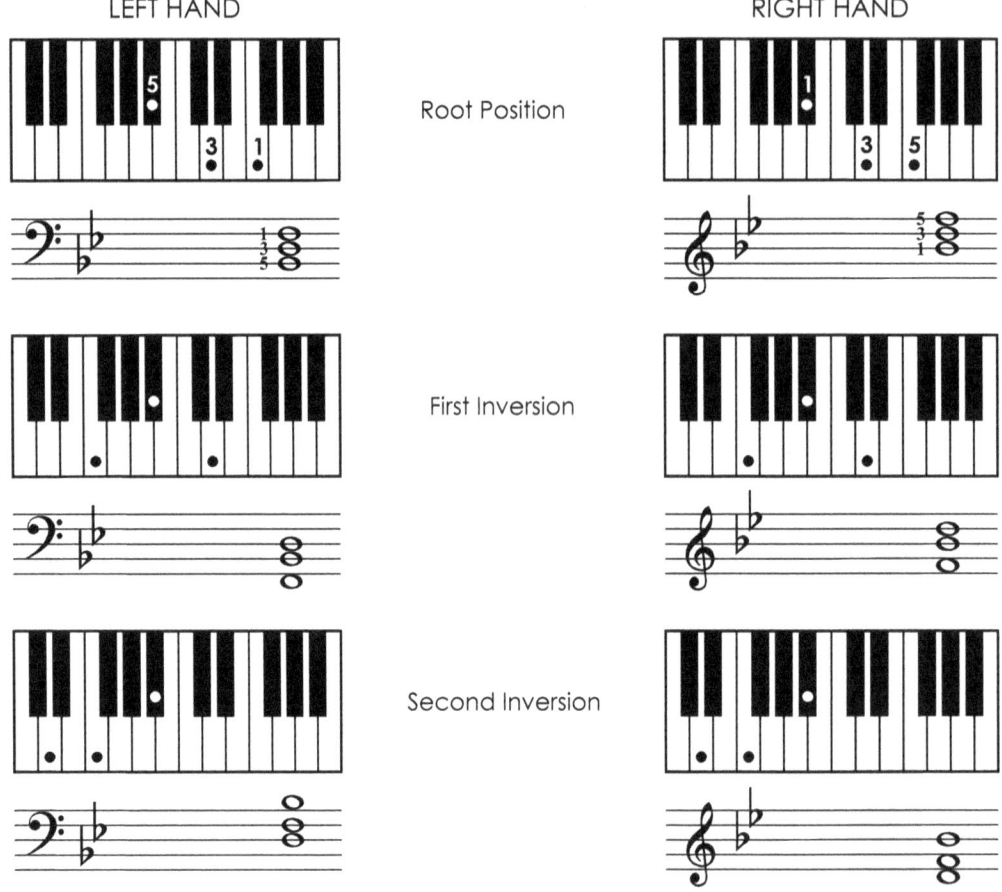

The two pictures below give examples of using both hands to play a chord. The two hand method produces a full or rich sound. Another purpose for the two hand method is to allow the hands to function in separate capacities. For example, the right hand can hold a chord while the left hand plays a pattern or the left hand can hold a chord while the right hand plays a melody, etc.

BOTH HANDS

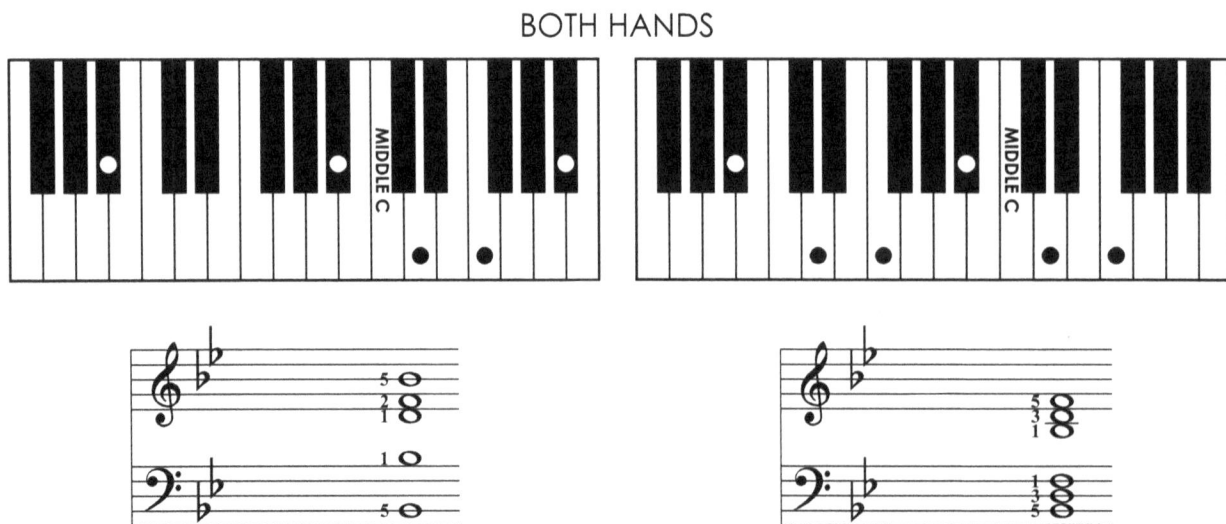

Major Scales, Major Chords & Exercises - B♭ Major

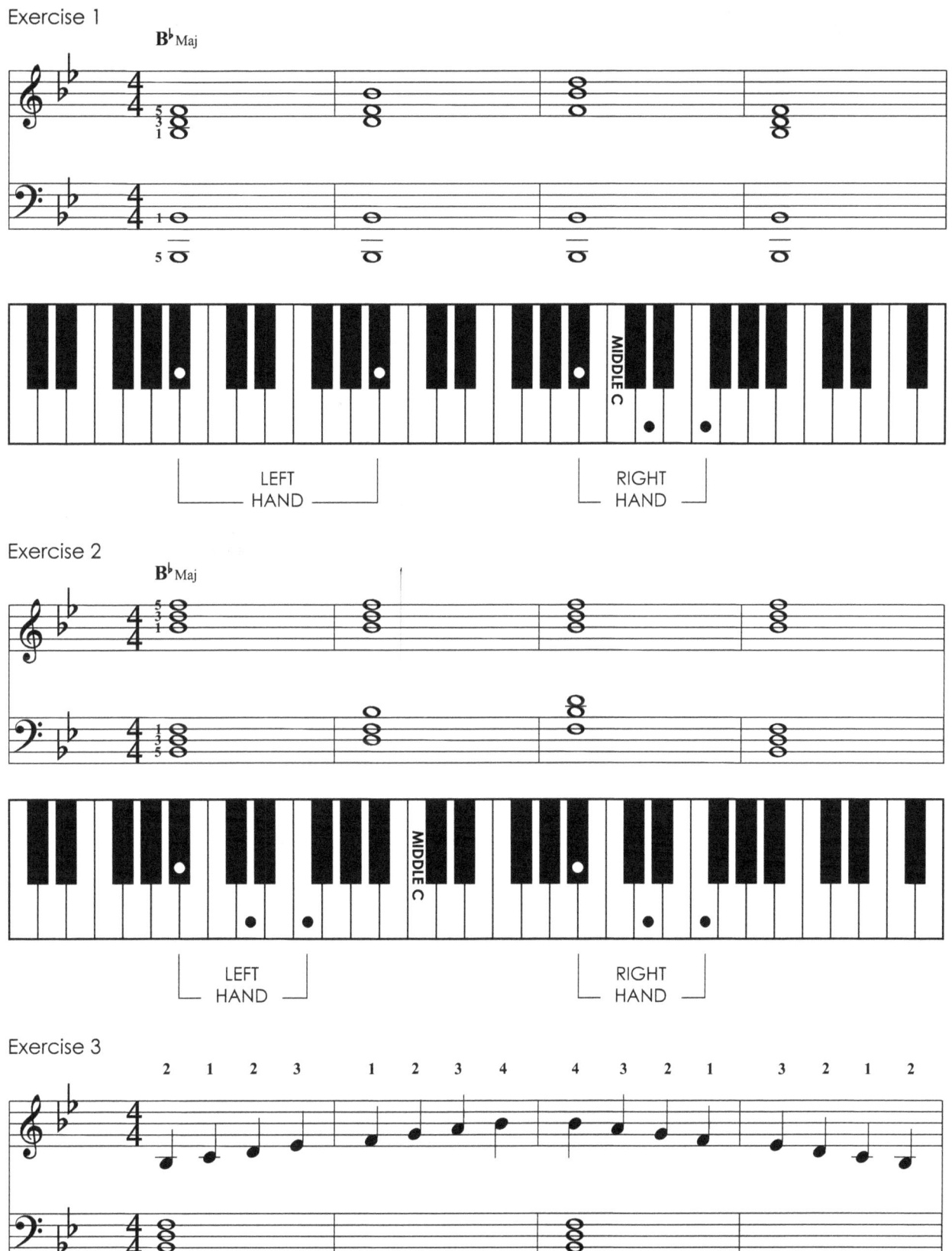

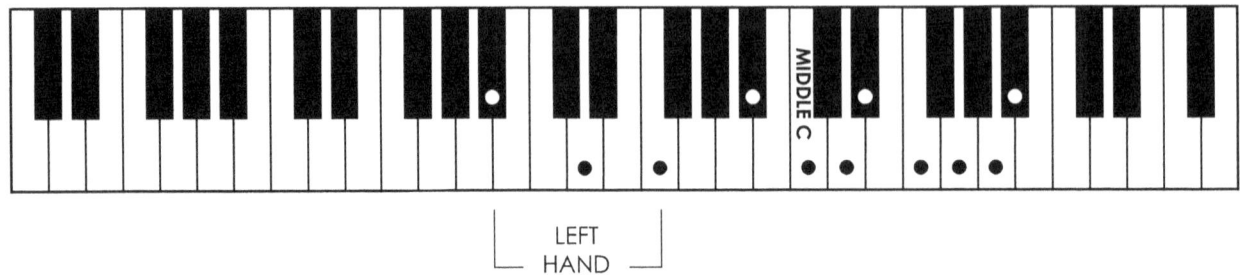

Exercise 4

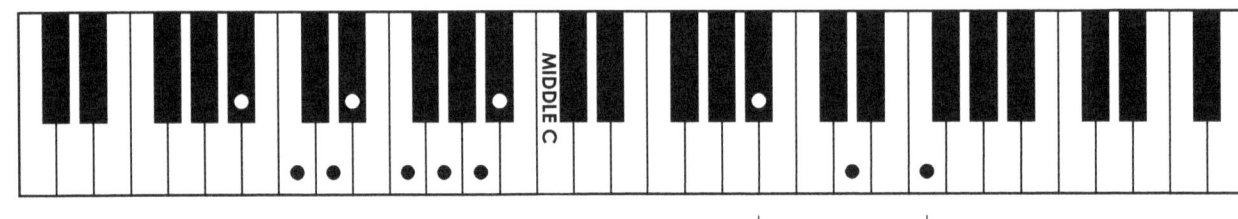

Exercise 5

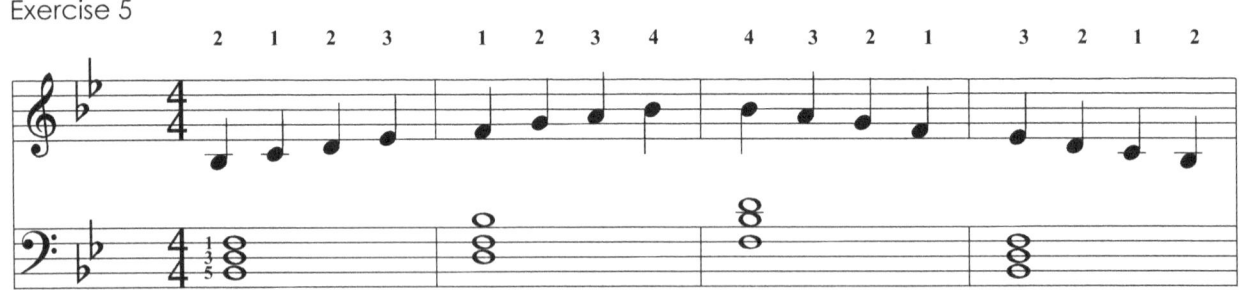

Exercise 6

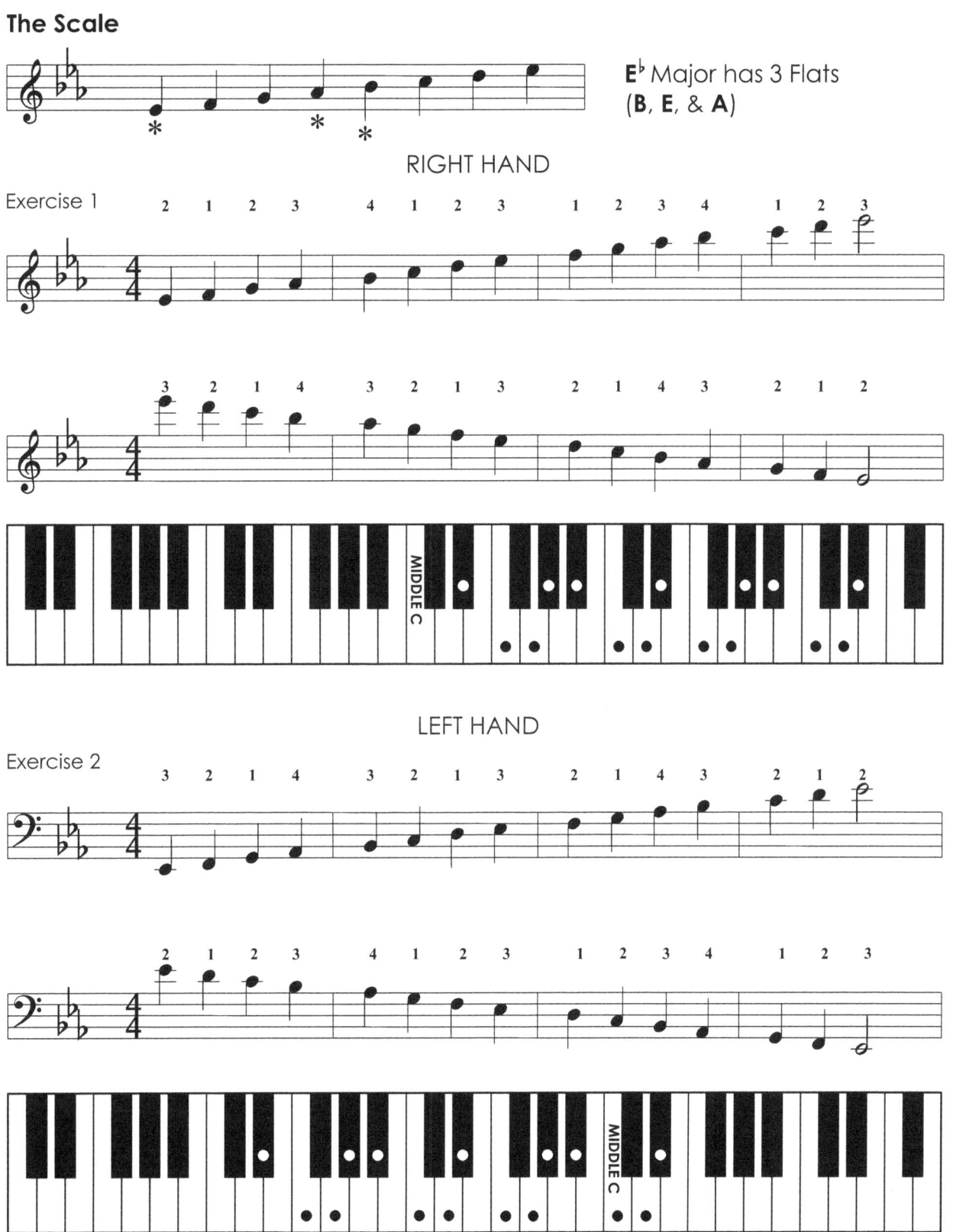

Major Scales, Major Chords & Exercises - E♭ Major

BOTH HANDS

Exercise 3

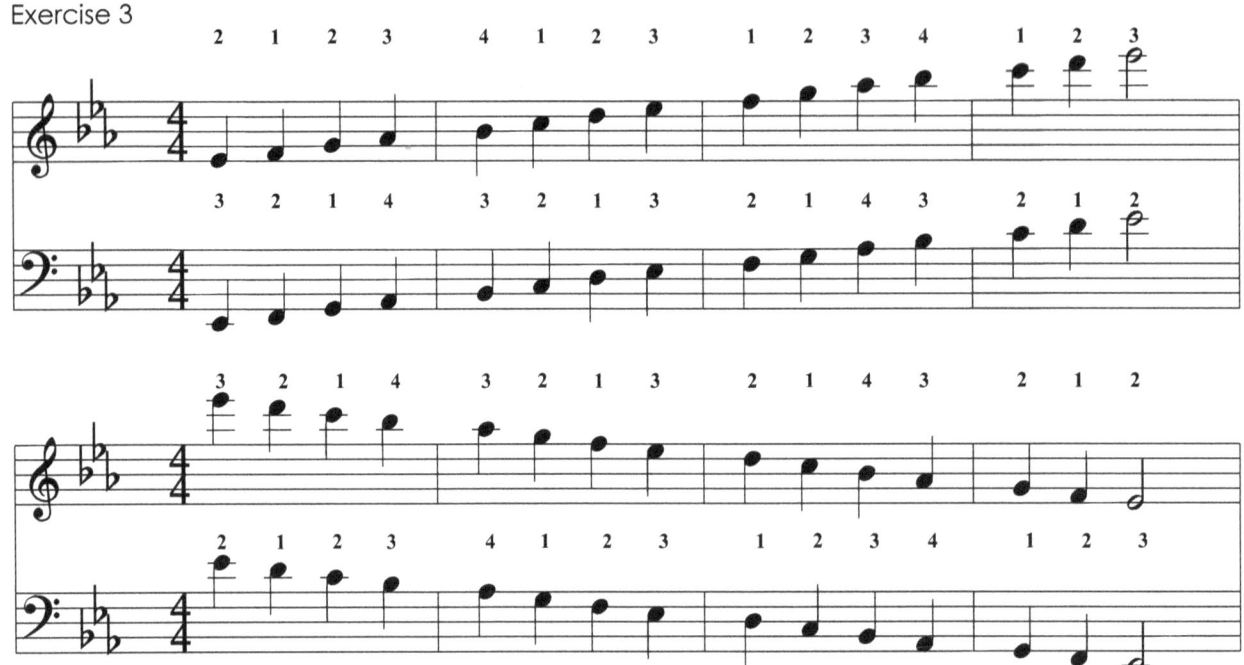

The Chord

The written symbol for the E♭ Major chord is '**E♭**Maj'.

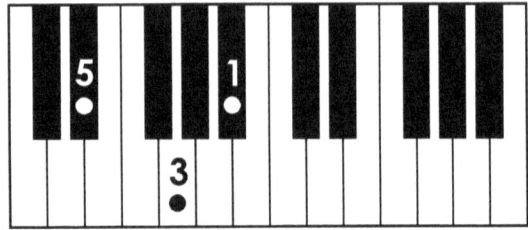

The Left Hand holding **E♭ Major** chord with numbers 5, 3 and 1 fingers.

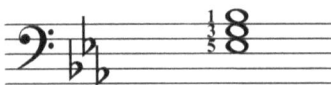

The **E♭ Major** chord written on the Stave (Bass Clef).

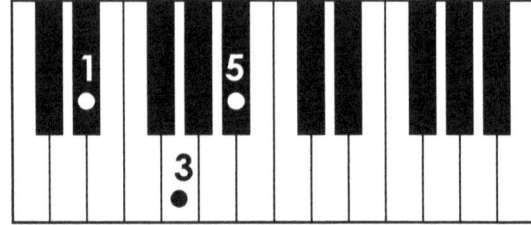

The Right Hand holding **E♭ Major** chord with numbers 1, 3 and 5 fingers.

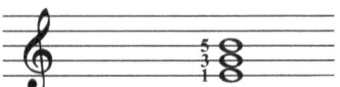

The **E♭ Major** chord written on the Stave (Treble Clef).

Major chords can be played in three different positions. These positions are called Inversions. It is not always possible to hold an inverted chord with numbers 1, 3 and 5 fingers, numbers 2 or 4 fingers may be substituted as needed.

Major Scales, Major Chords & Exercises - E♭ Major

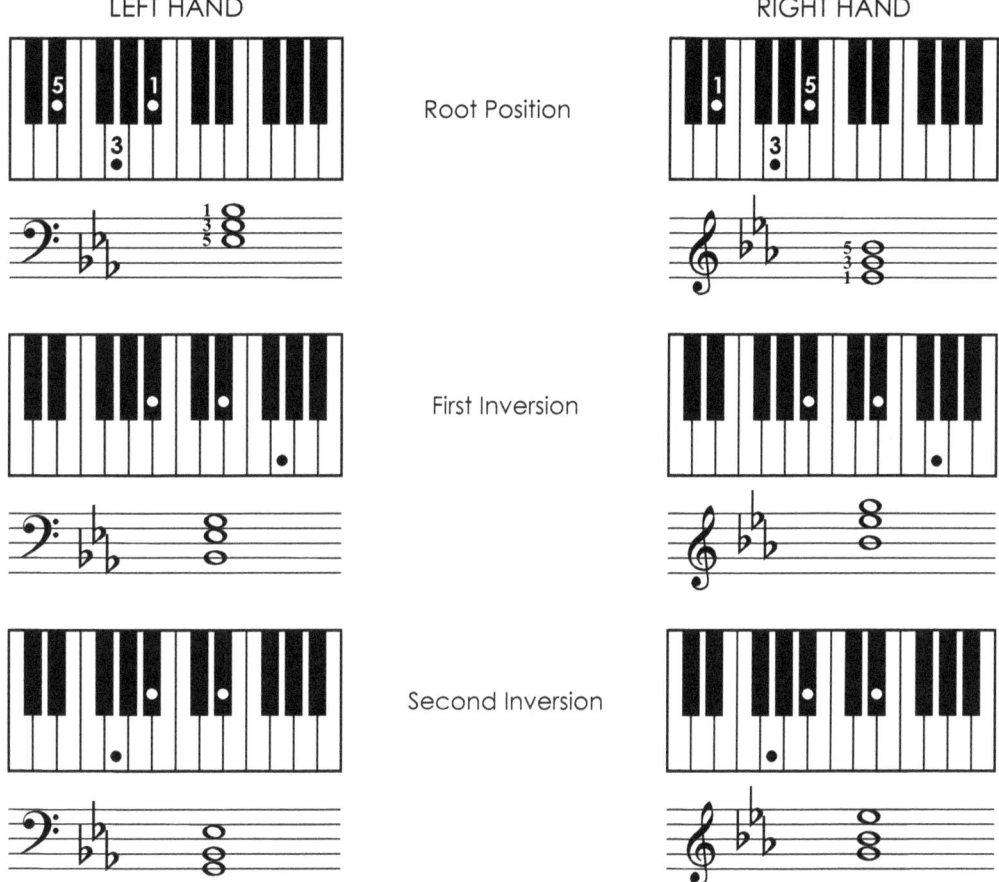

The two pictures below give examples of using both hands to play a chord. The two hand method produces a full or rich sound. Another purpose for the two hand method is to allow the hands to function in separate capacities. For example, the right hand can hold a chord while the left hand plays a pattern or the left hand can hold a chord while the right hand plays a melody, etc.

BOTH HANDS

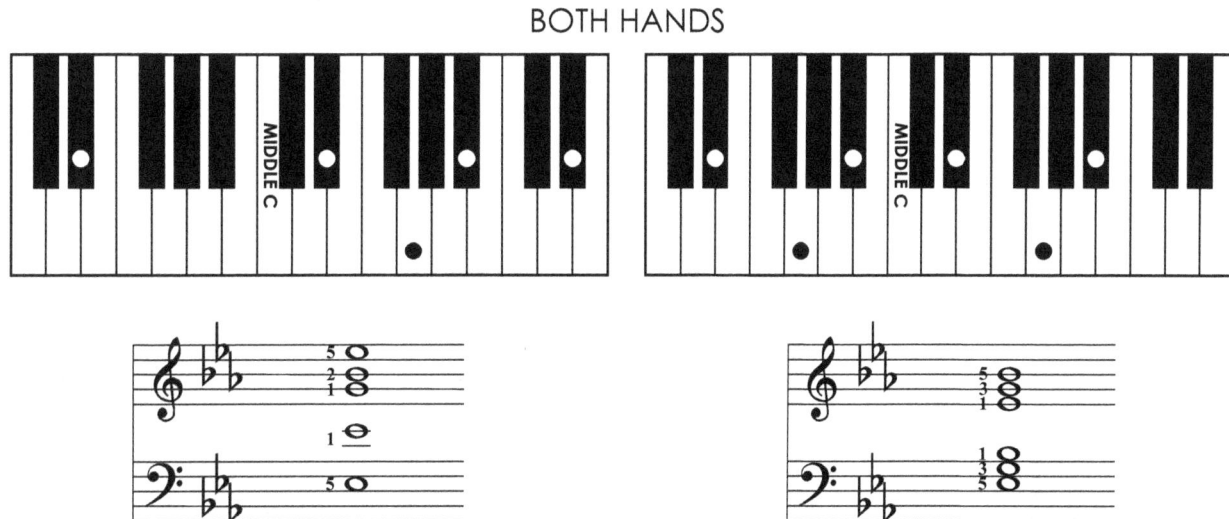

Major Scales, Major Chords & Exercises - E♭ Major

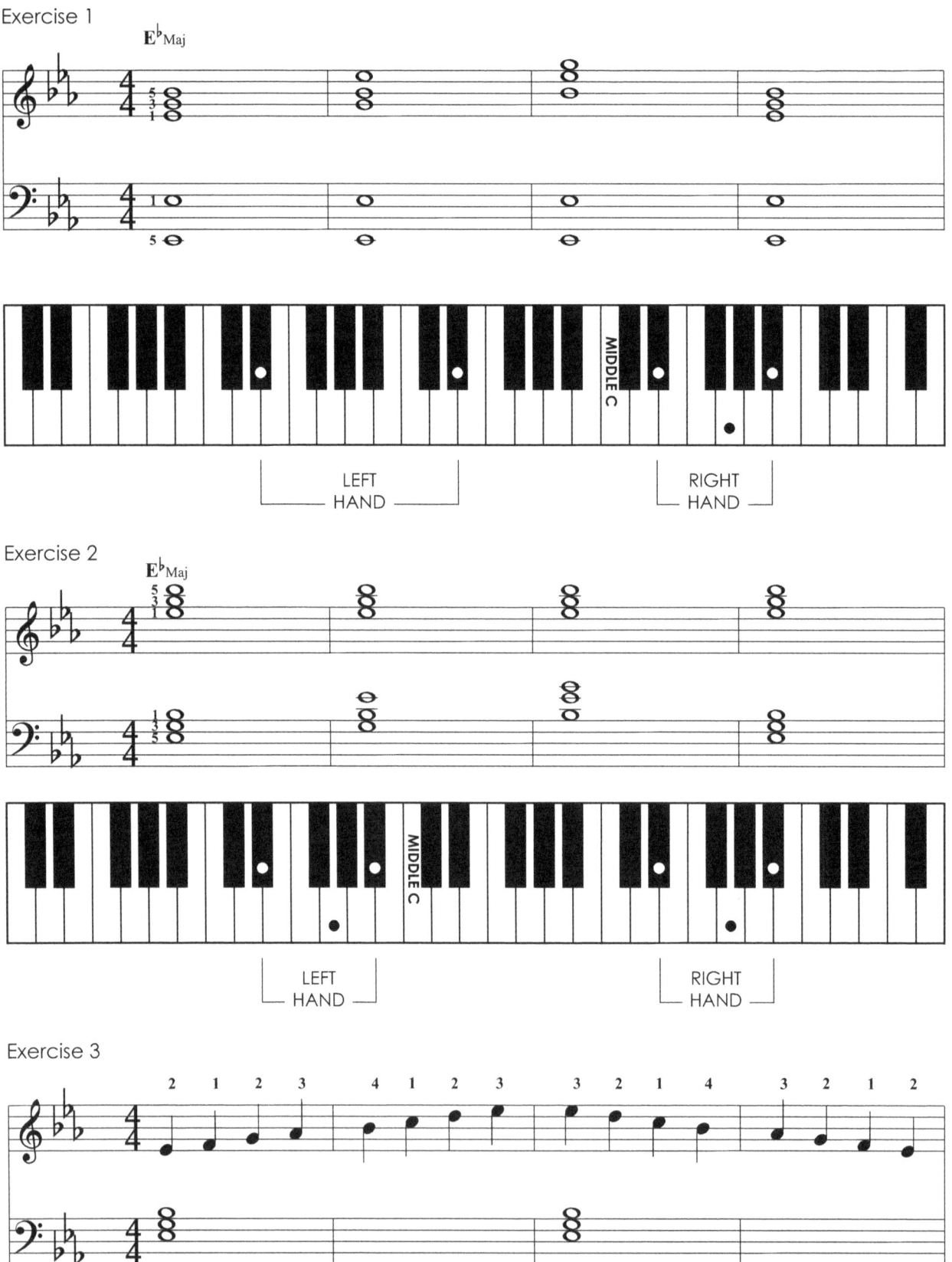

Major Scales, Major Chords & Exercises - E♭ Major

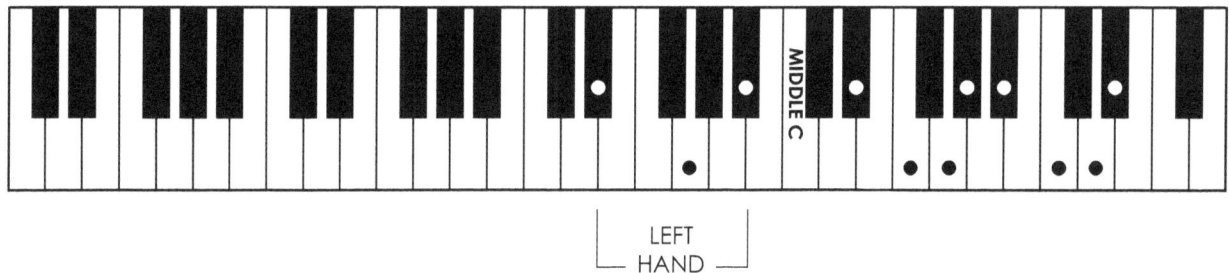

Exercise 4

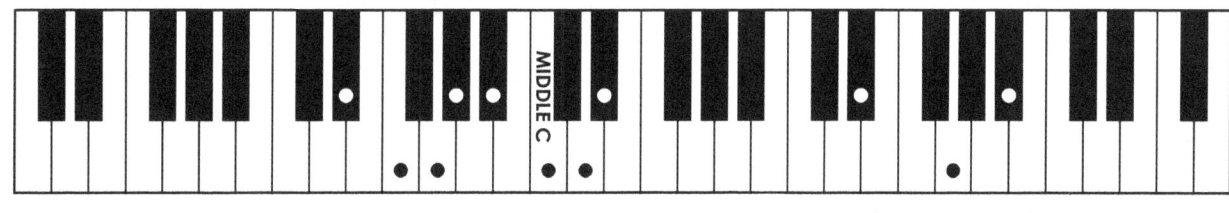

Exercise 5

Exercise 6

The Key of A♭ Major

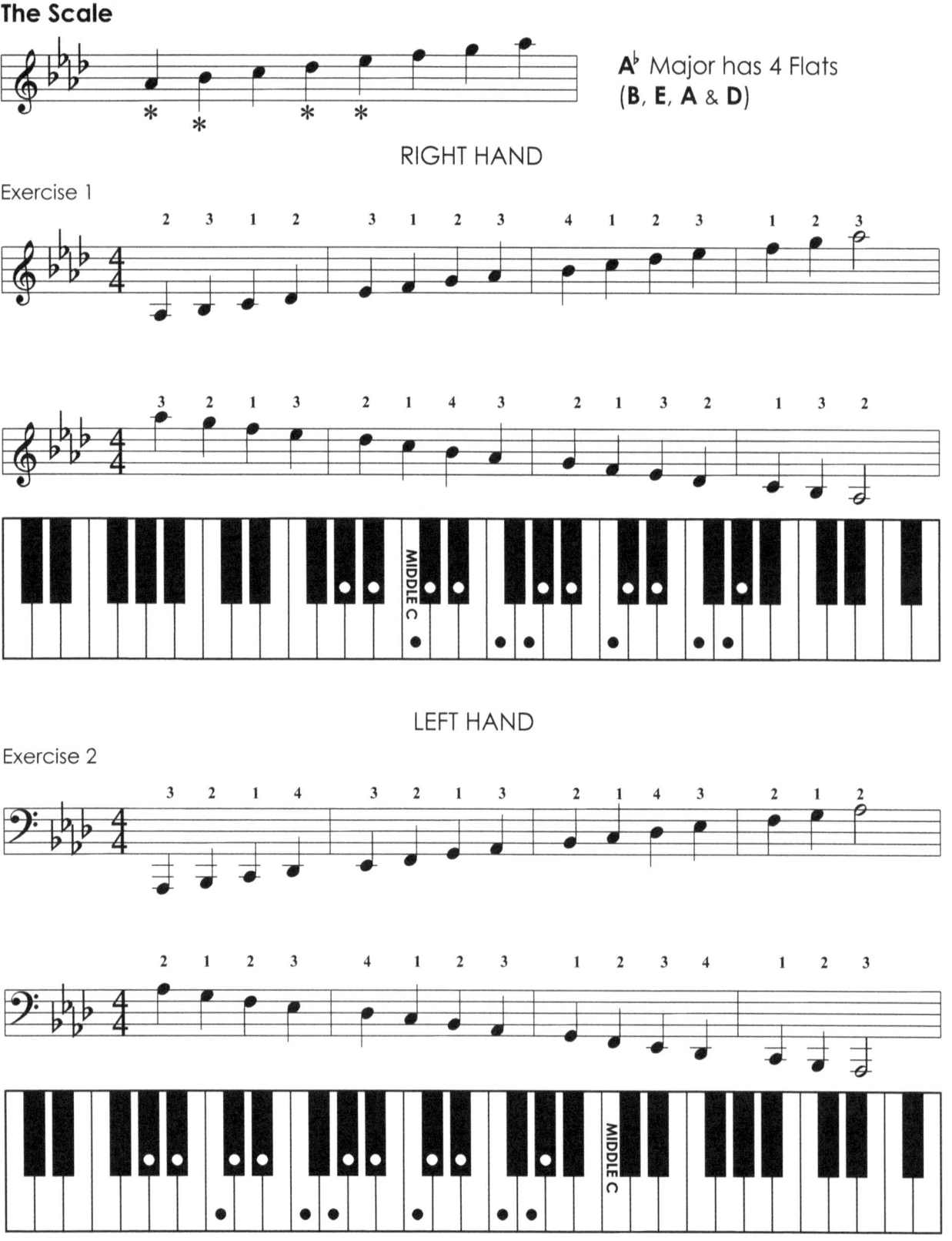

Major Scales, Major Chords & Exercises - A♭ Major

BOTH HANDS

Exercise 3

The Chord

The written symbol for the A♭ Major chord is '**A♭Maj**'.

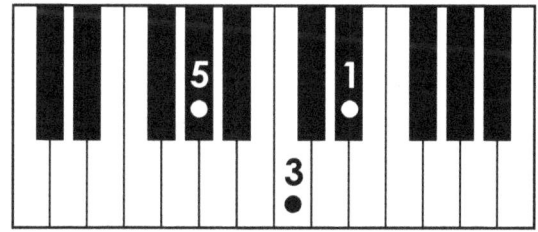

The Left Hand holding **A♭ Major** chord with numbers 5, 3 and 1 fingers.

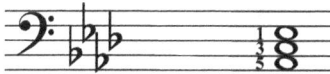

The **A♭ Major** chord written on the Stave (Bass Clef).

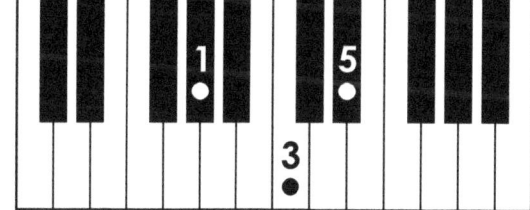

The Right Hand holding **A♭ Major** chord with numbers 1, 3 and 5 fingers.

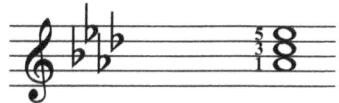

The **A♭ Major** chord written on the Stave (Treble Clef).

Major chords can be played in three different positions. These positions are called Inversions. It is not always possible to hold an inverted chord with numbers 1, 3 and 5 fingers, numbers 2 or 4 fingers may be substituted as needed.

65

Major Scales, Major Chords & Exercises - A♭ Major

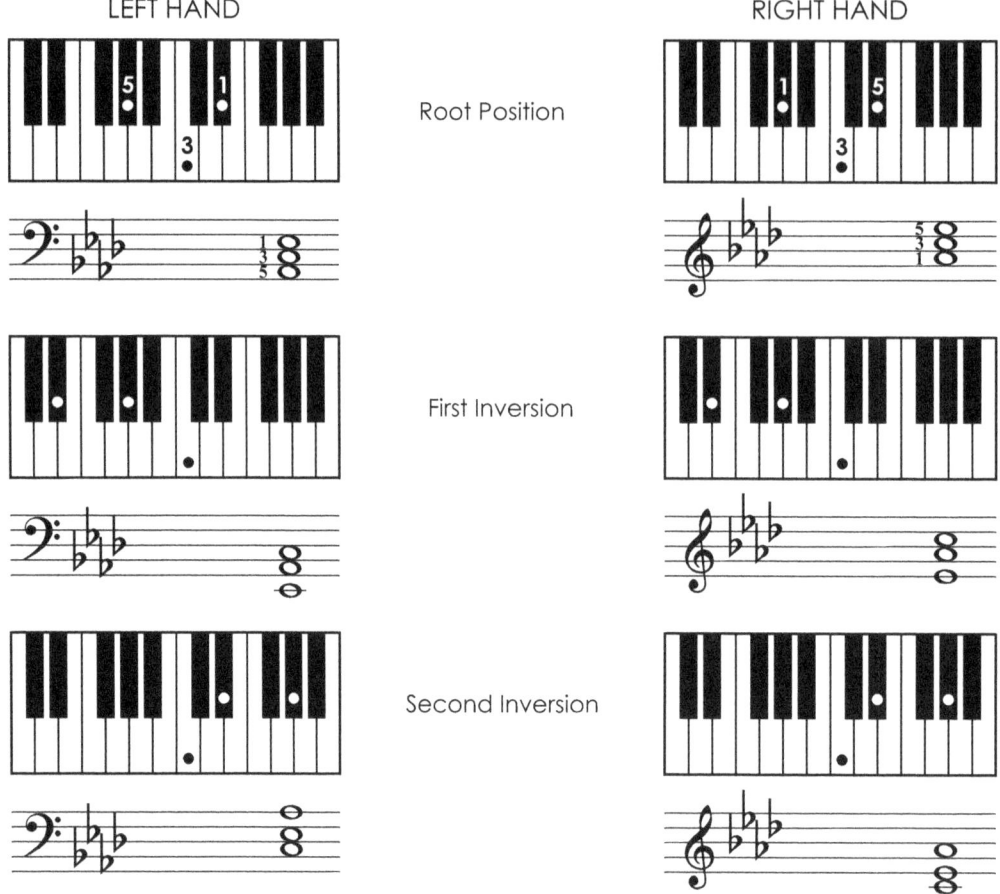

The two pictures below give examples of using both hands to play a chord. The two hand method produces a full or rich sound. Another purpose for the two hand method is to allow the hands to function in separate capacities. For example, the right hand can hold a chord while the left hand plays a pattern or the left hand can hold a chord while the right hand plays a melody, etc.

BOTH HANDS

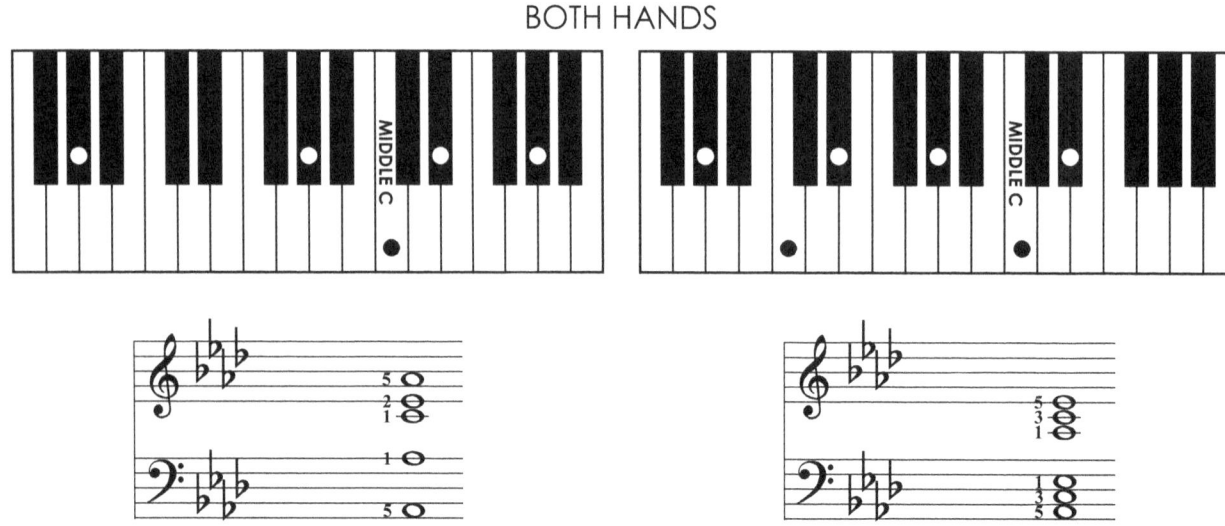

Major Scales, Major Chords & Exercises - A♭ Major

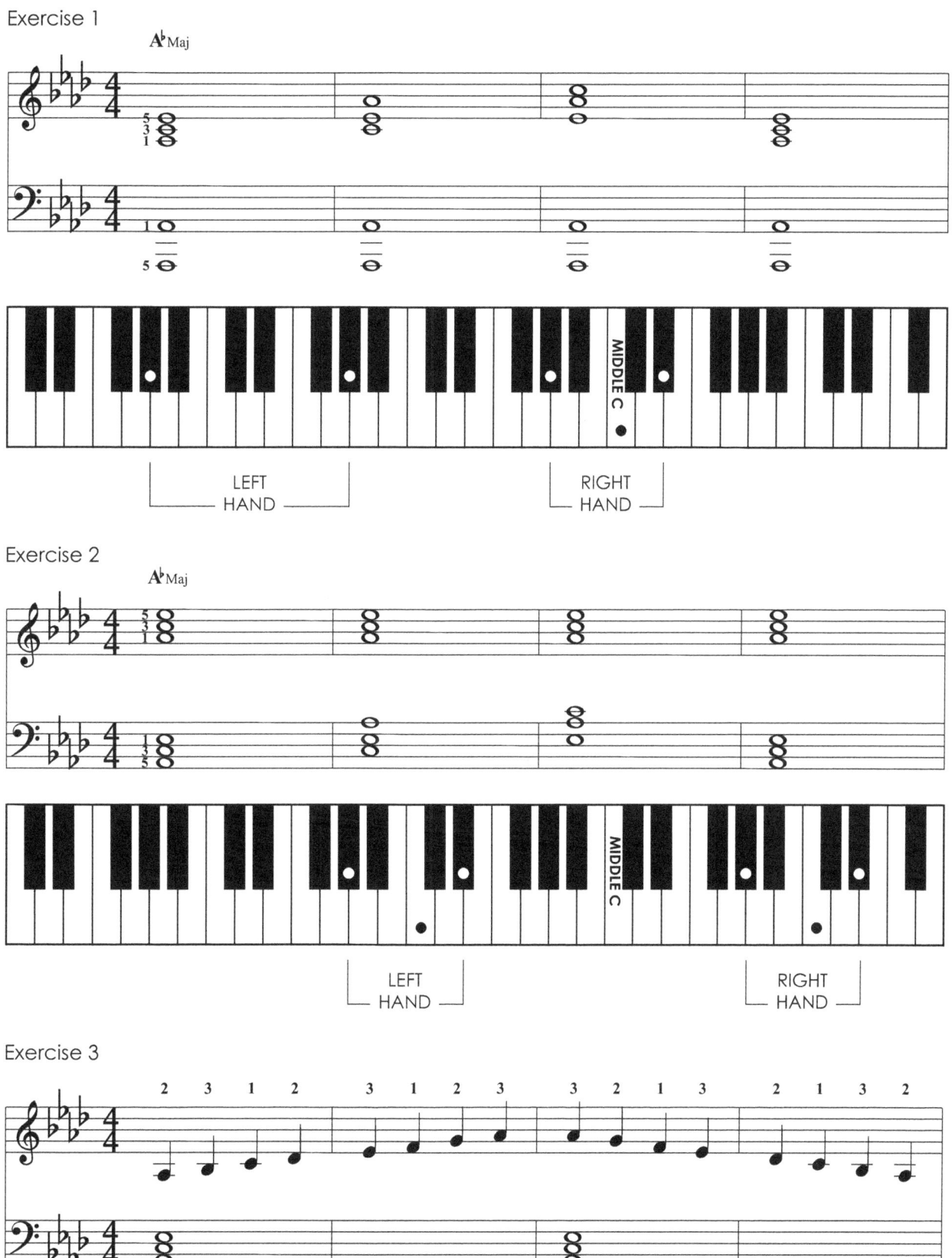

Major Scales, Major Chords & Exercises - A♭ Major

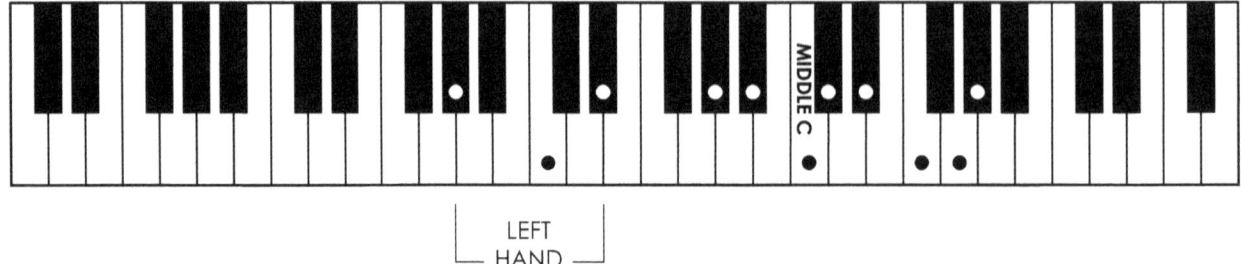

LEFT HAND

Exercise 4

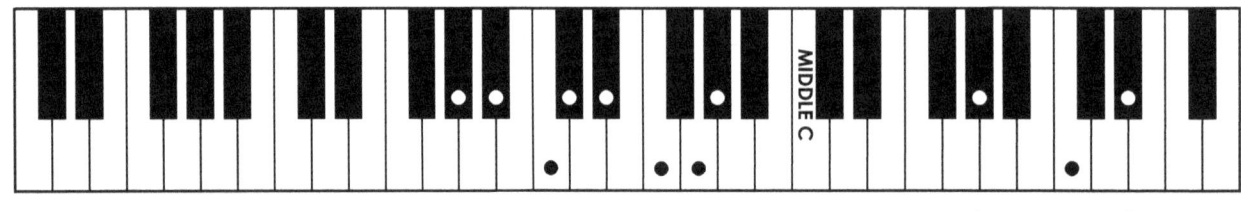

RIGHT HAND

Exercise 5

Exercise 6

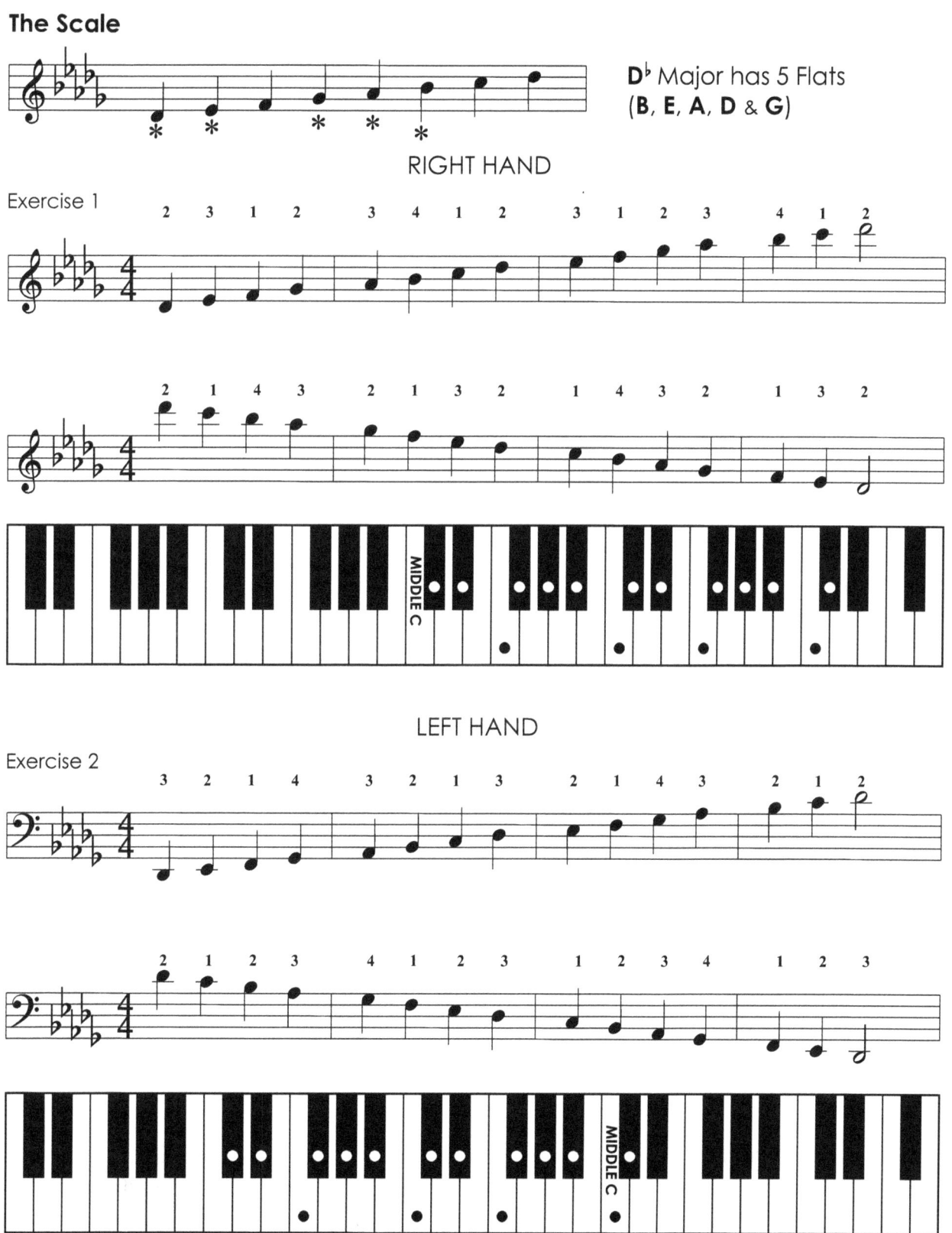

Major Scales, Major Chords & Exercises - D♭ Major

BOTH HANDS

Exercise 3

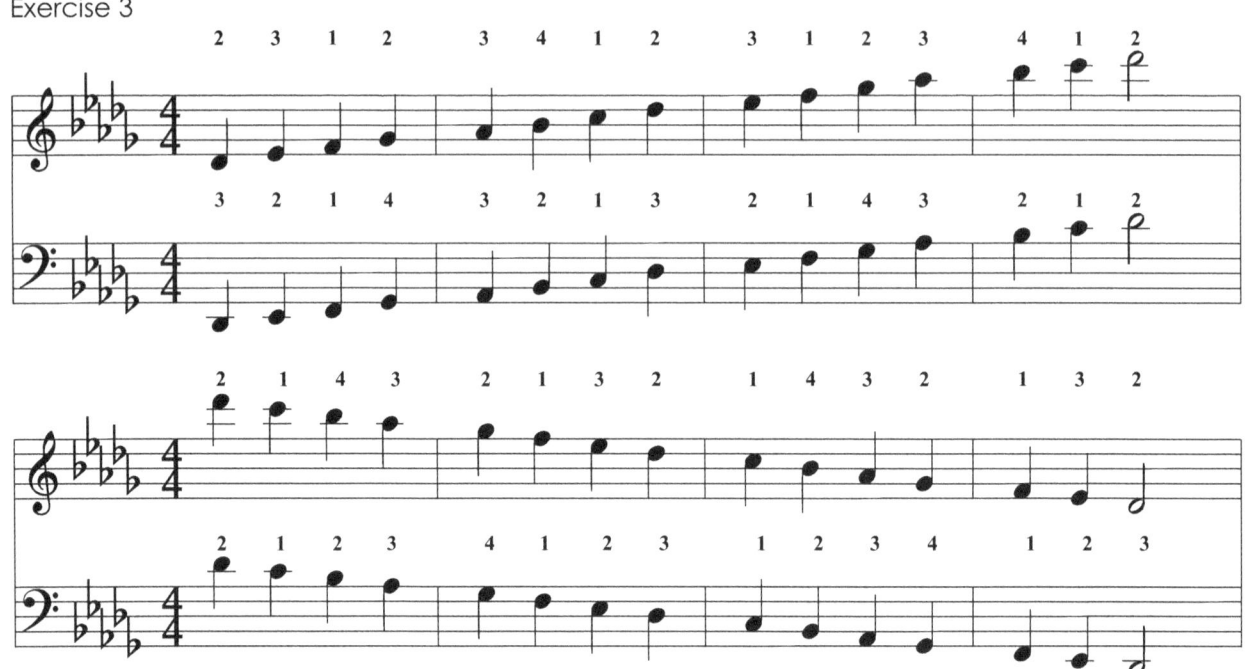

The Chord

The written symbol for the D♭ Major chord is '**D♭** Maj'.

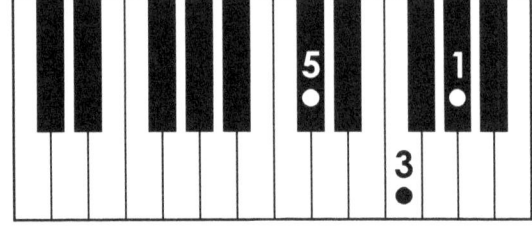

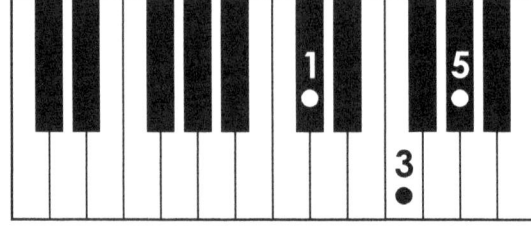

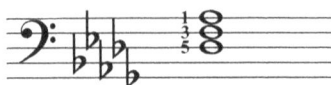

The Left Hand holding **D♭ Major** chord with numbers 5, 3 and 1 fingers.

The Right Hand holding **D♭ Major** chord with numbers 1, 3 and 5 fingers.

The **D♭ Major** chord written on the Stave (Bass Clef).

The **D♭ Major** chord written on the Stave (Treble Clef).

Major chords can be played in three different positions. These positions are called Inversions. It is not always possible to hold an inverted chord with numbers 1, 3 and 5 fingers, numbers 2 or 4 fingers may be substituted as needed.

Major Scales, Major Chords & Exercises - D♭ Major

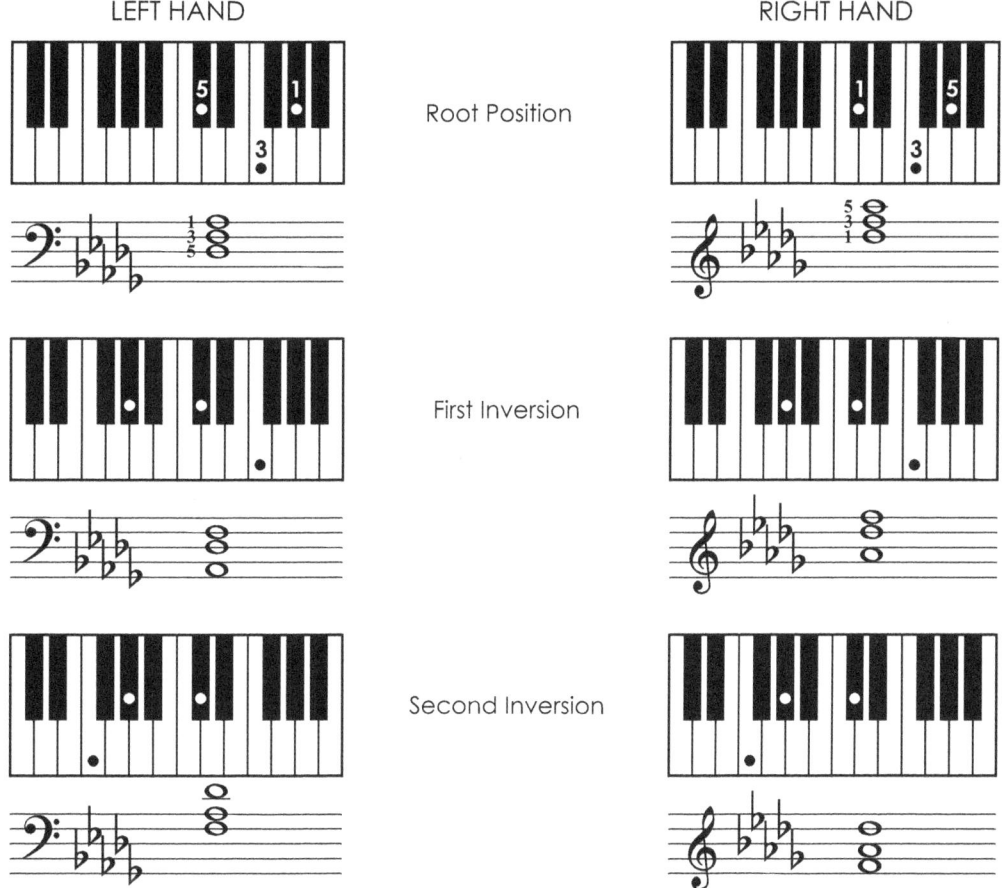

The two pictures below give examples of using both hands to play a chord. The two hand method produces a full or rich sound. Another purpose for the two hand method is to allow the hands to function in separate capacities. For example, the right hand can hold a chord while the left hand plays a pattern or the left hand can hold a chord while the right hand plays a melody, etc.

BOTH HANDS

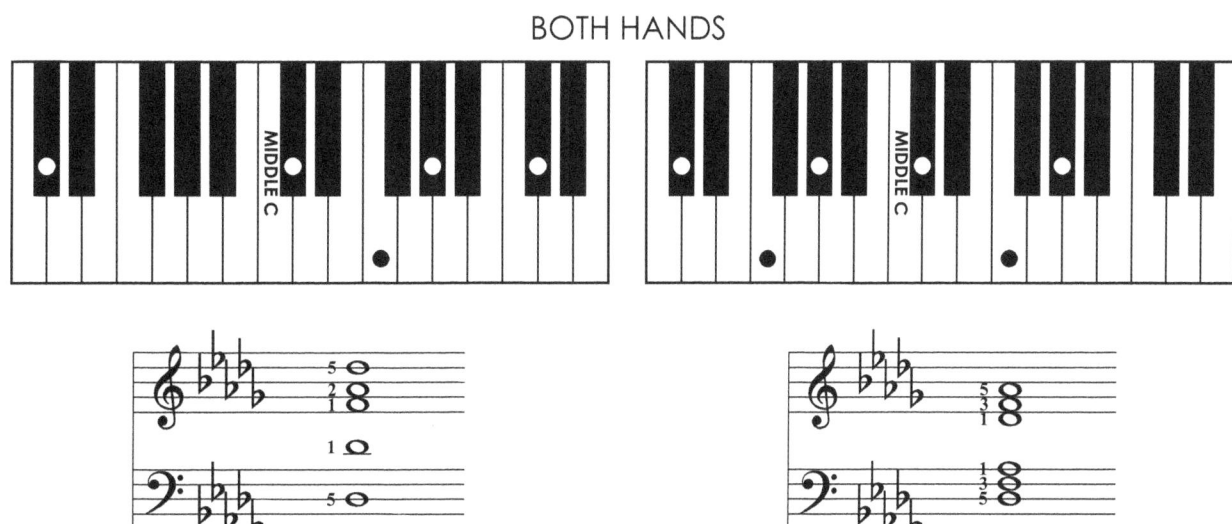

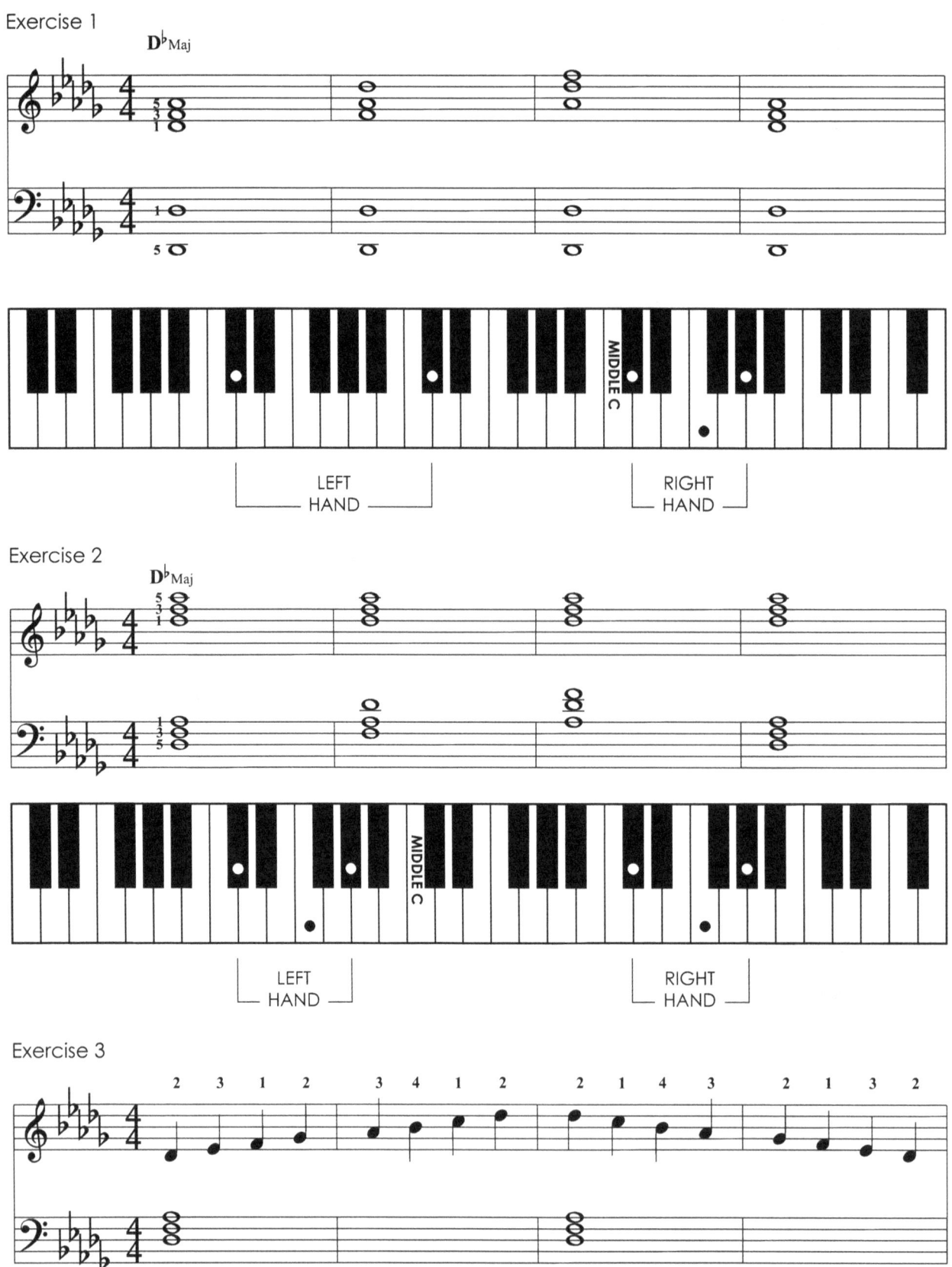

Major Scales, Major Chords & Exercises - *D♭ Major*

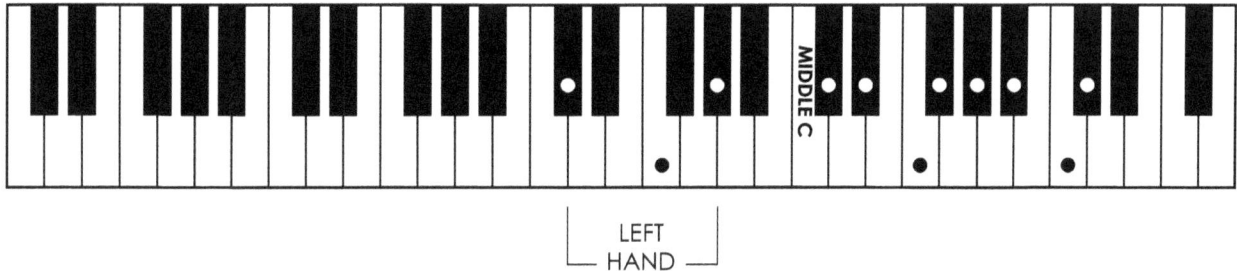

Exercise 4

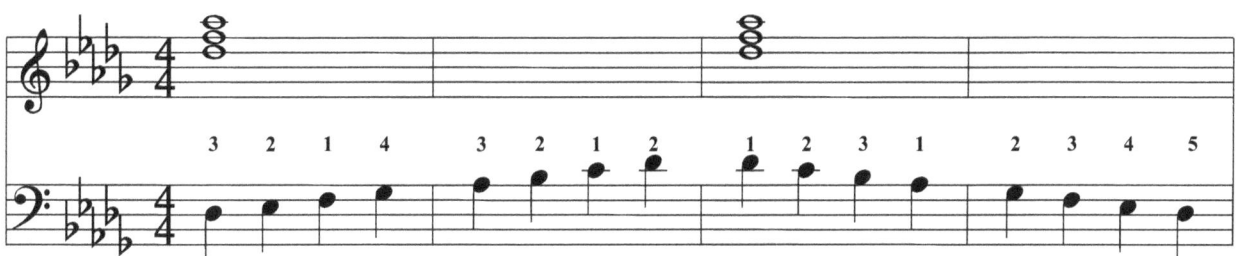

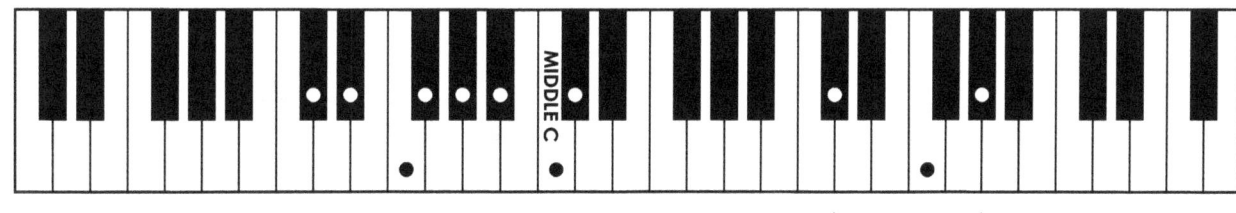

Exercise 5

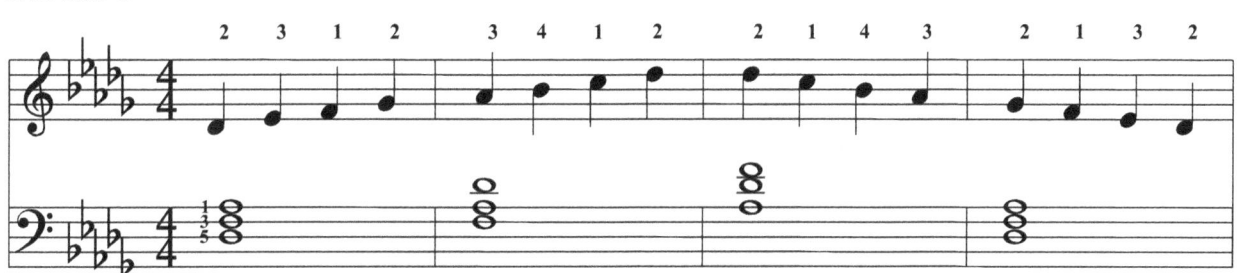

Exercise 6

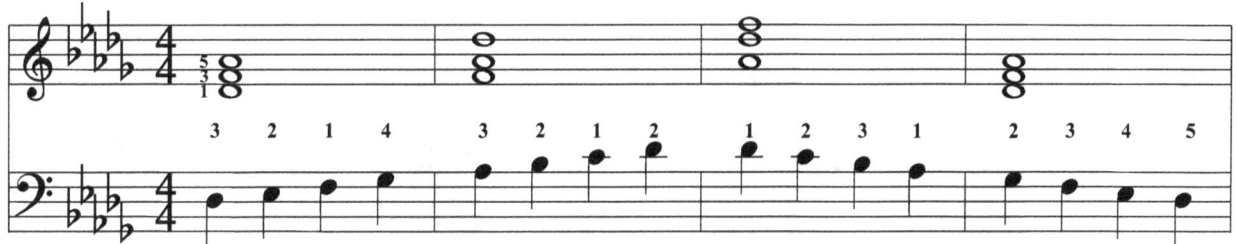

73

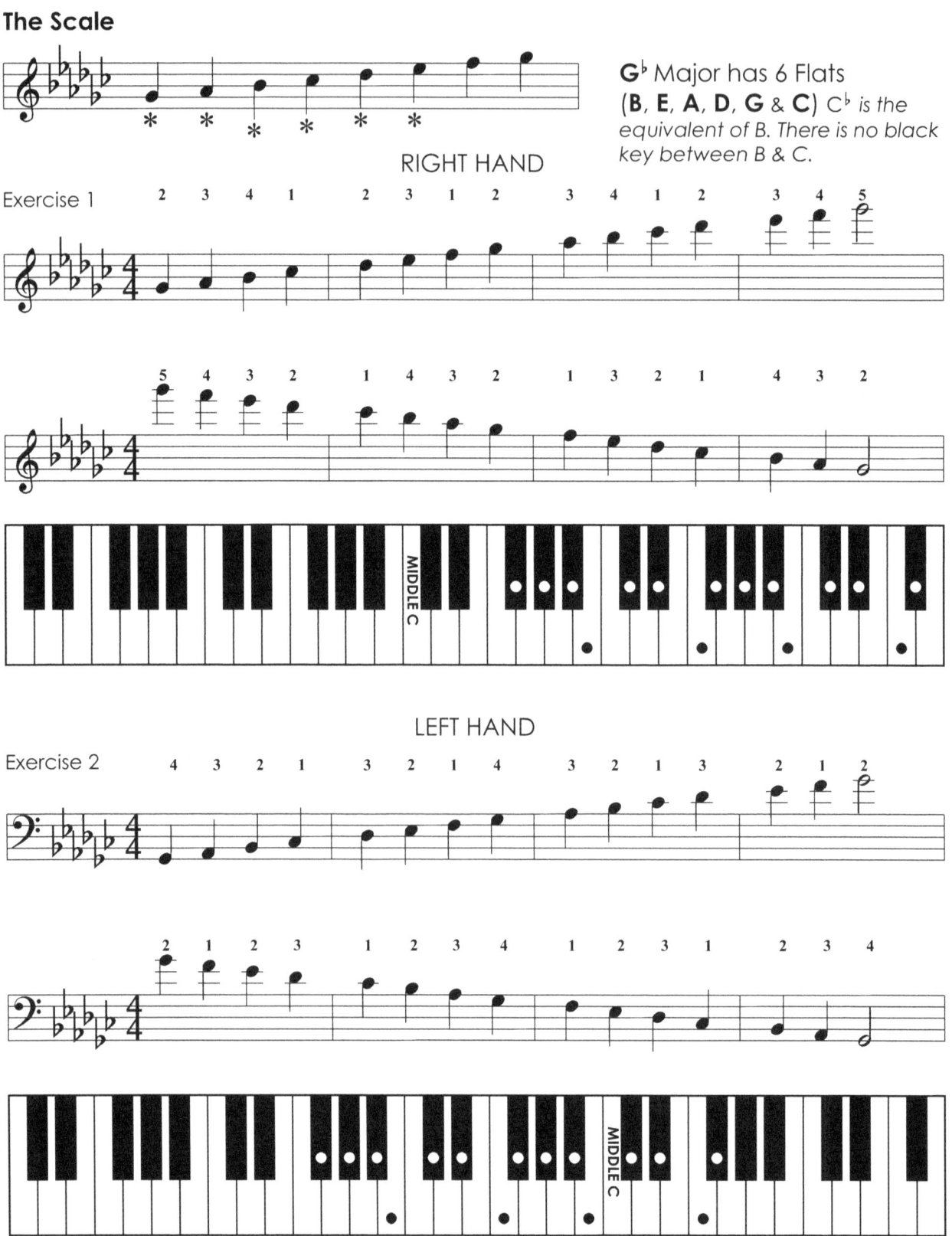

Major Scales, Major Chords & Exercises - G♭ Major

BOTH HANDS

Exercise 3

The Chord

The written symbol for the G♭ Major chord is '**G♭**Maj'.

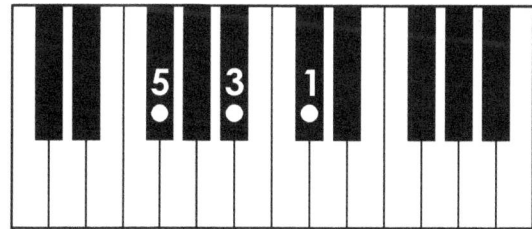

The Left Hand holding **G♭ Major** chord with numbers 5, 3 and 1 fingers.

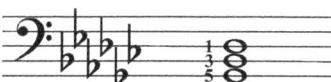

The **G♭ Major** chord written on the Stave (Bass Clef).

The Right Hand holding **G♭ Major** chord with numbers 1, 3 and 5 fingers.

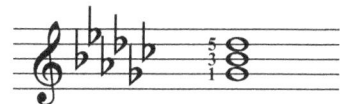

The **G♭ Major** chord written on the Stave (Treble Clef).

Major chords can be played in three different positions. These positions are called Inversions. It is not always possible to hold an inverted chord with numbers 1, 3 and 5 fingers, numbers 2 or 4 fingers may be substituted as needed.

75

Major Scales, Major Chords & Exercises - G♭ Major

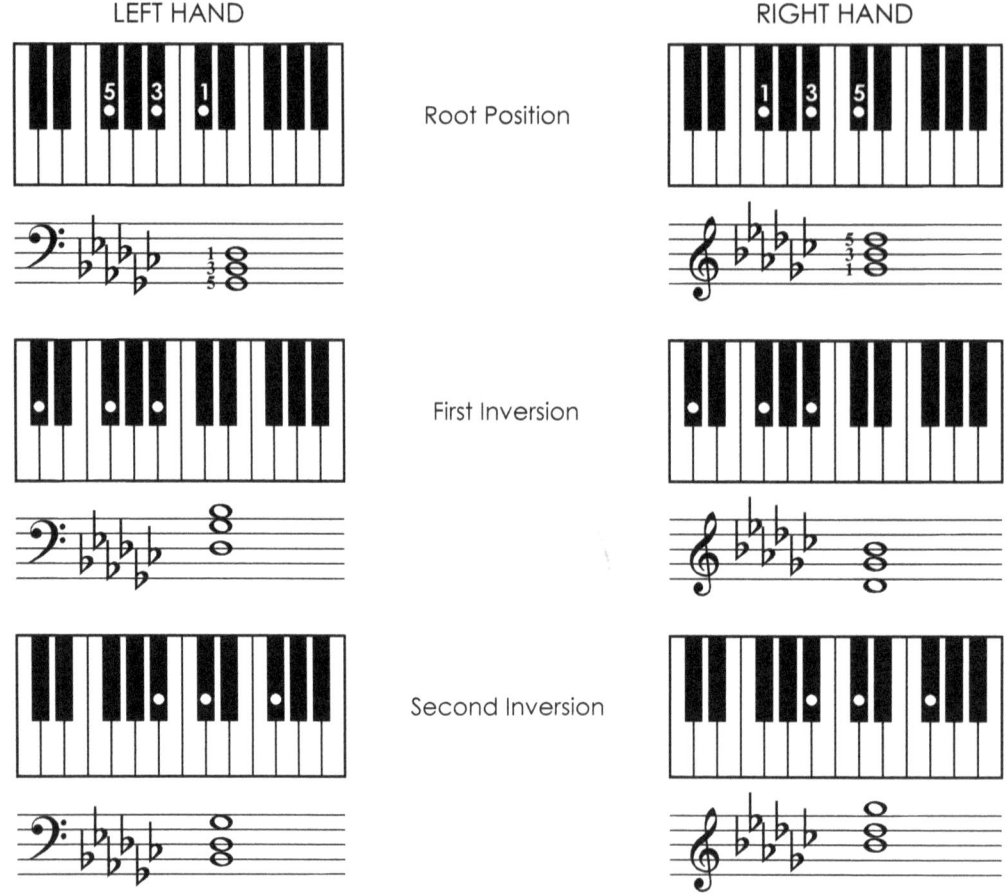

The two pictures below give examples of using both hands to play a chord. The two hand method produces a full or rich sound. Another purpose for the two hand method is to allow the hands to function in separate capacities. For example, the right hand can hold a chord while the left hand plays a pattern or the left hand can hold a chord while the right hand plays a melody, etc.

BOTH HANDS

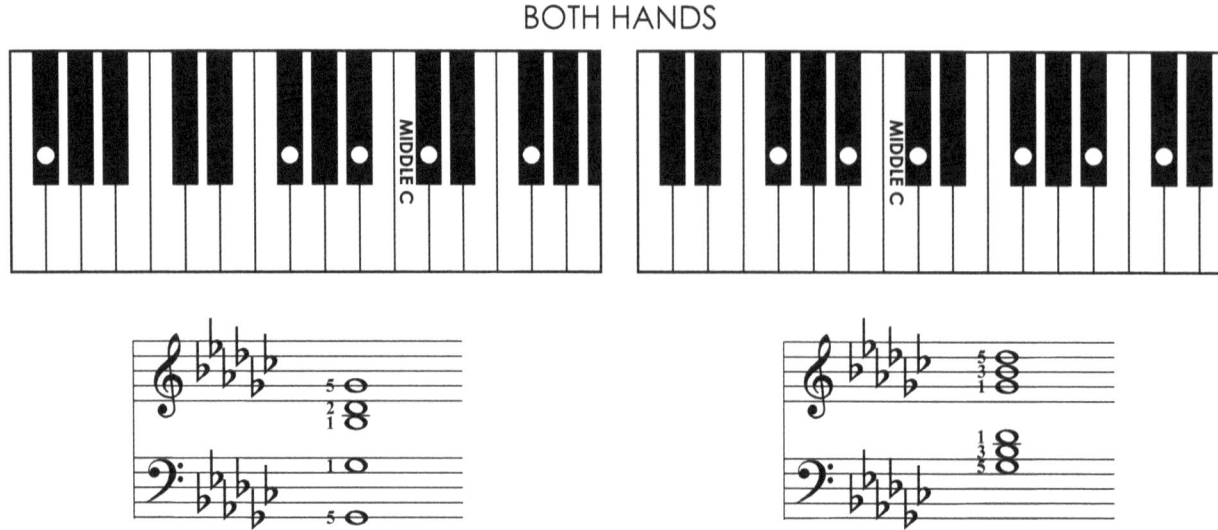

Major Scales, Major Chords & Exercises - G♭ Major

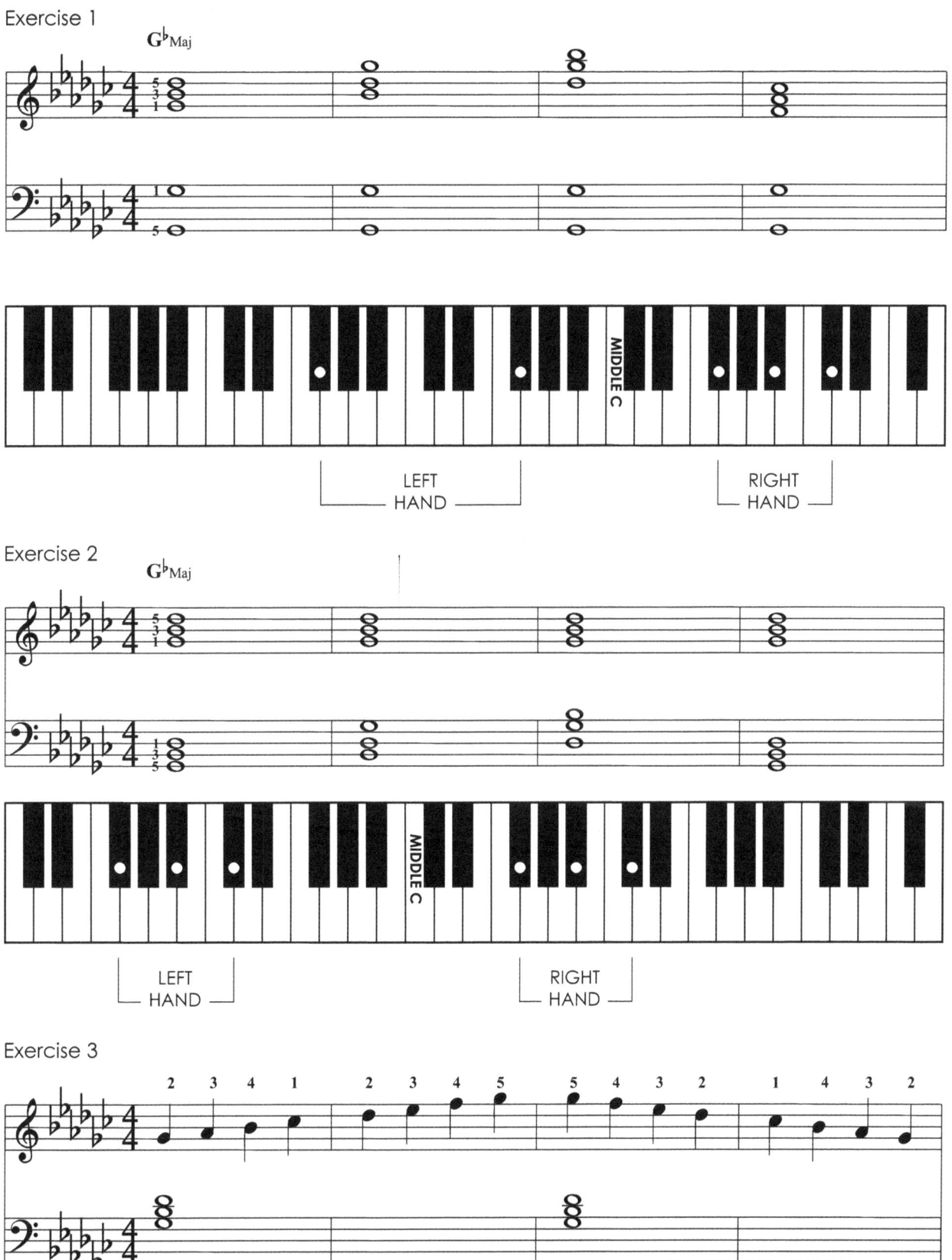

Major Scales, Major Chords & Exercises - G♭ Major

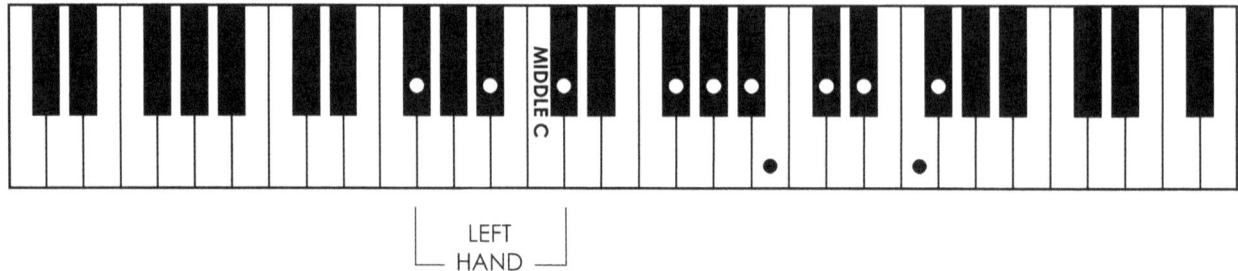

Exercise 4

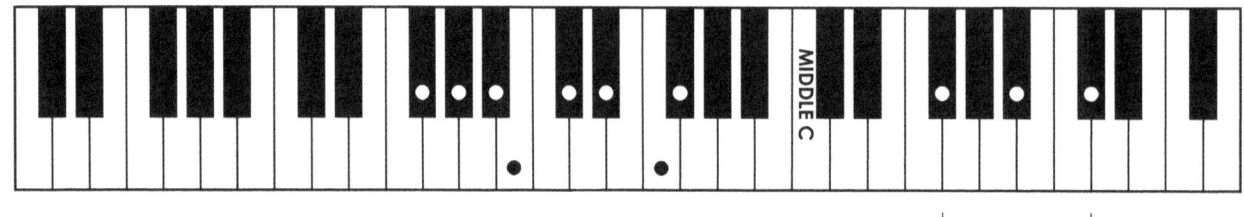

Exercise 5

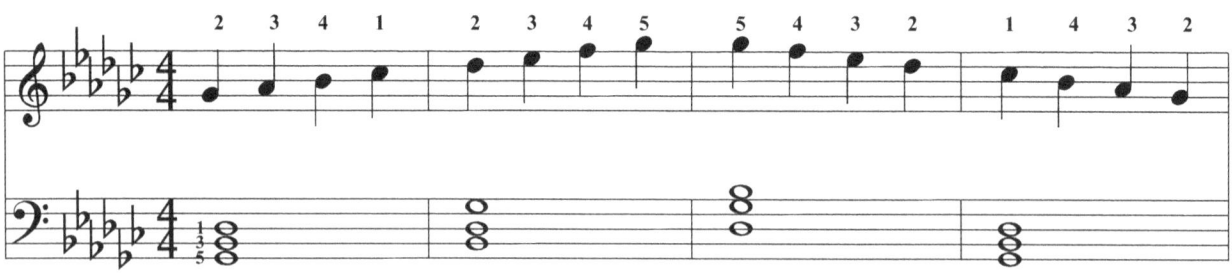

Exercise 6

Chapter 6

Families of Chords

Playing songs require the musician to play in a Key. Now that we have completed all the previous exercises I'm sure you have realized there are 12 Keys. As a beginner I want to introduce you to the basic approach to playing a song.

Each Key has a family or group of Chords that is used to accompany or harmonize with a melody.

The following diagrams show the 12 Keys and the basic group of Chords that are used. These groups are most frequently used together.

Within the Key the number of the Chords are the First, Fourth and Fifth, which are indicated or written in Roman Numerals as I, IV & V (1,4 & 5). This will be explained further in the Intermediate Book.

The Chords are members of families, just like you and I. Most all of us have a family of some kind, and we have immediate family, cousins, etc. We see our immediate family more than we see our cousins. It's like that in music, too.

Think of the 3 Chords in each family group as the immediate family. The immediate family Chords I, IV, and V, are used much more frequently in songs.

You can experiment by singing songs or listening to songs and play along using the Chords in a family group. It may not sound great at first but you will get it eventually.

In the key of C Major - C, F & G are used

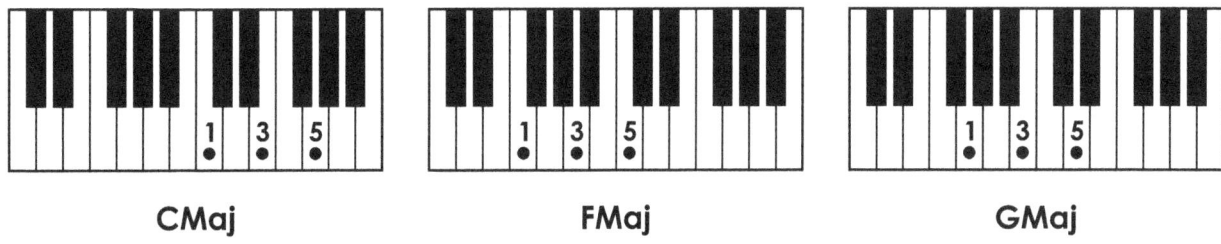

In the key of G Major - G, C & D are used

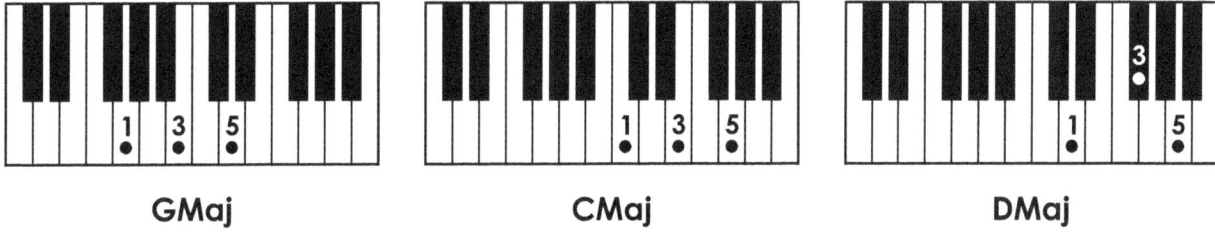

In the key of D Major - D, G & A are used

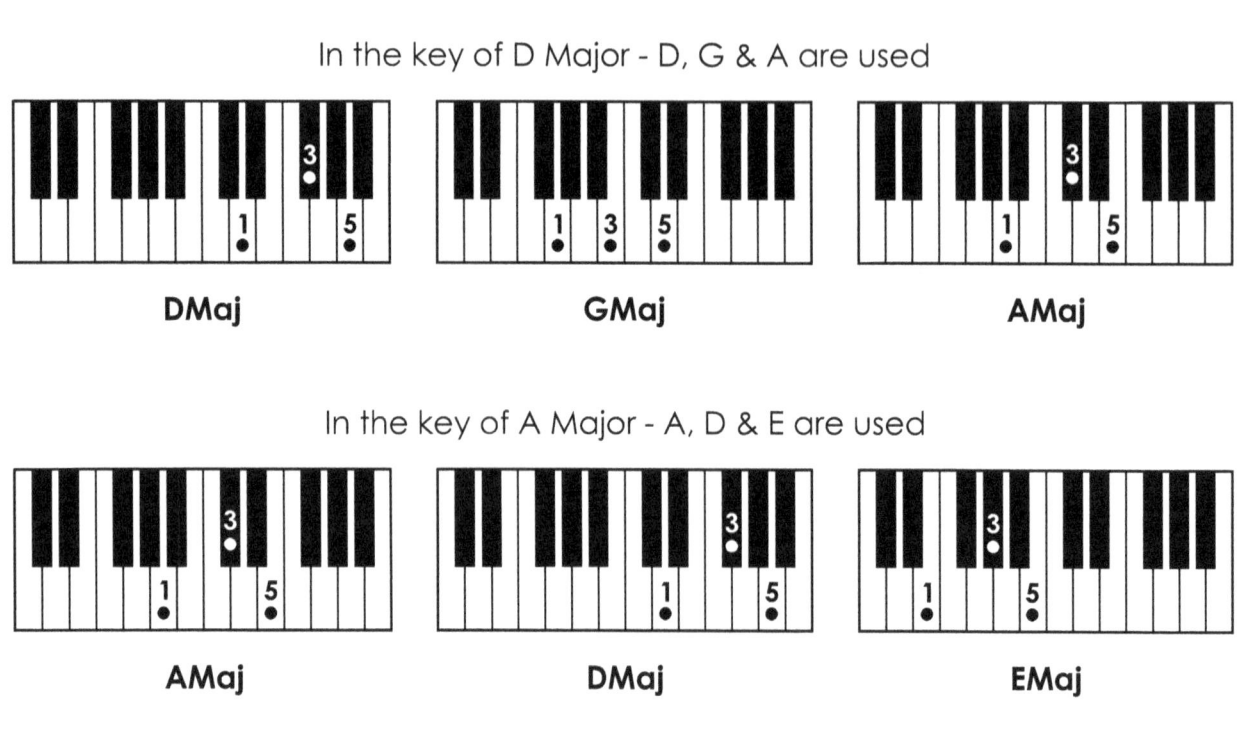

In the key of A Major - A, D & E are used

In the key of E Major - E, A & B are used

In the key of B Major - B, E & F# are used

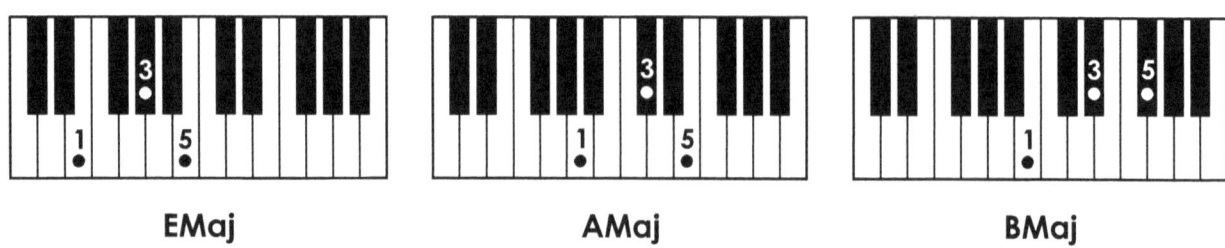

In the key of F Major - F, B♭ & C are used

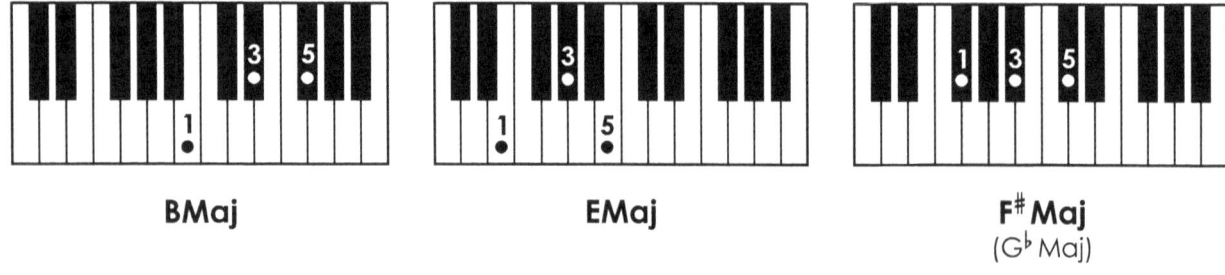

In the key of B♭ Major - B♭, E♭ & F are used

B♭Maj 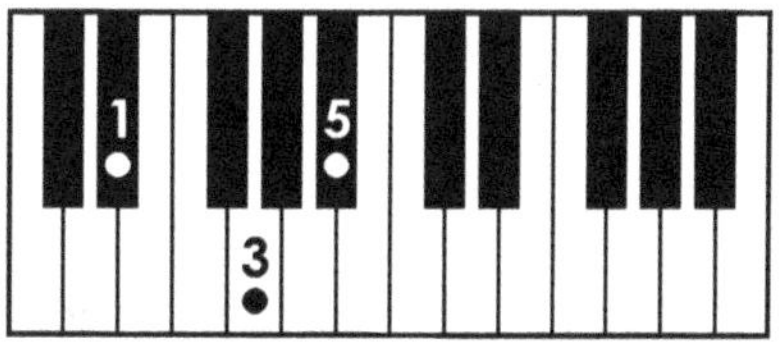   **E♭Maj** 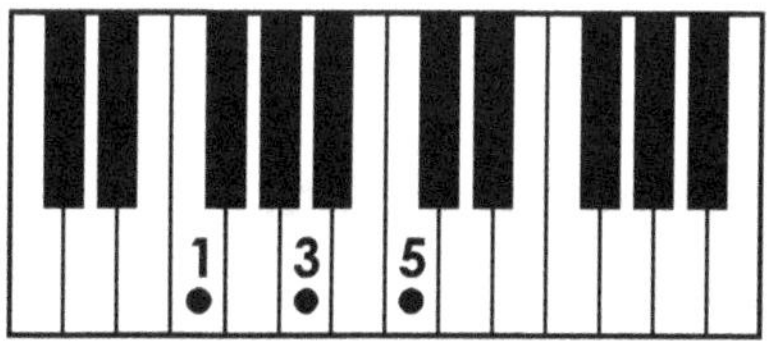   **FMaj**

In the key of E♭ Major - E♭, A♭ & B♭ are used

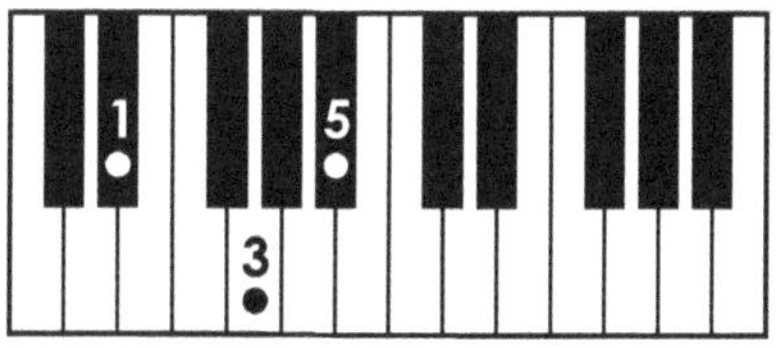

E♭Maj 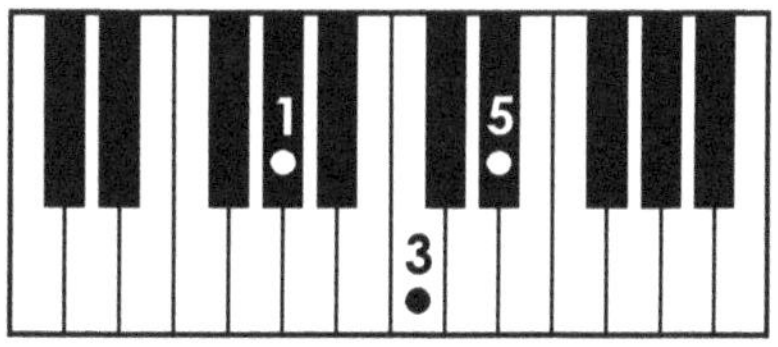   **A♭Maj**    **B♭Maj**

In the key of A♭ Major - A♭, D♭ & E♭ are used

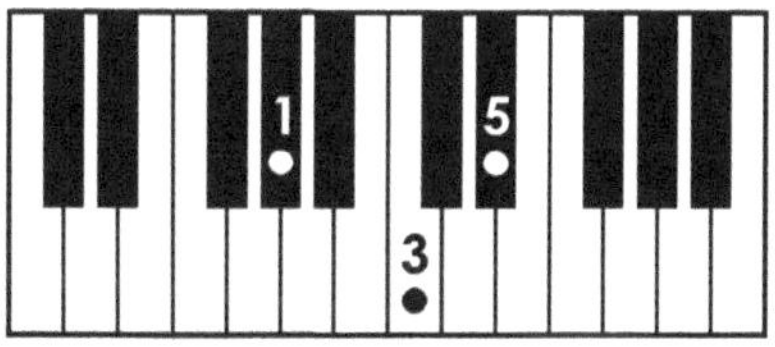

A♭Maj    **D♭Maj**    **E♭Maj**

In the key of D♭ Major - D♭, G♭ & A♭ are used

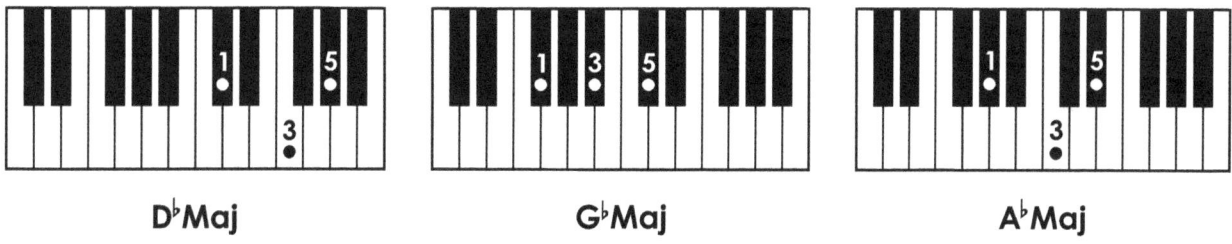

D♭Maj   **G♭Maj**   **A♭Maj**

In the key of G♭ Major - G♭, B & D♭ are used

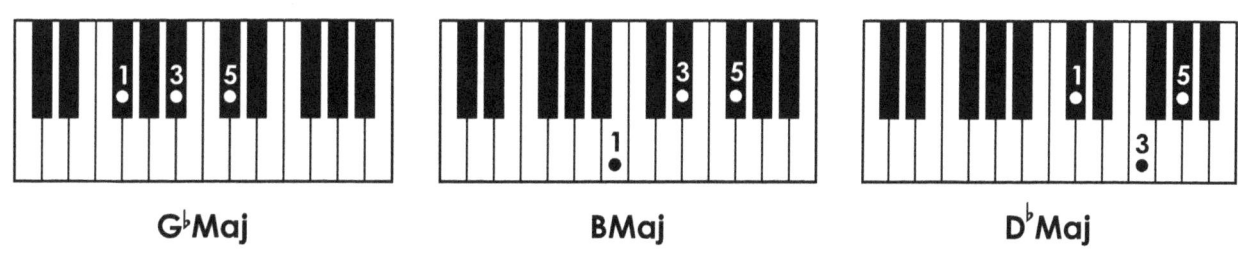

G♭Maj   **BMaj**   **D♭Maj**

Chapter 7

Playing Songs

Performance Tips

I hope that you read and studied all the material up to this point with great diligence and excitement. If you did, then here is where you will test your knowledge and understanding. If you are doubtful, I suggest that you go through the chapters or areas that you have trouble with.
If you are confident and ready to challenge yourself, then let's get started!

Before you attempt to play the songs, there are four important things I want you to practice. These can be adopted for any approach to playing musical pieces.

1. Identify the 'Key' of the musical piece.

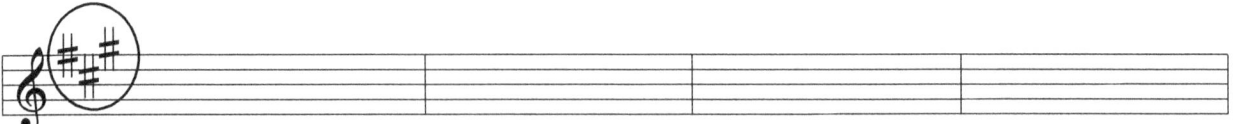

2. Identify the 'Time' of the musical piece.

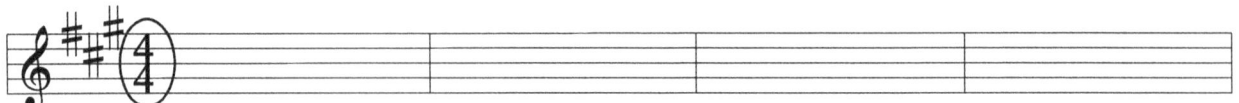

3. Clap or tap the rhythm, while paying attention to **ALL** signs, symbols and instructions.

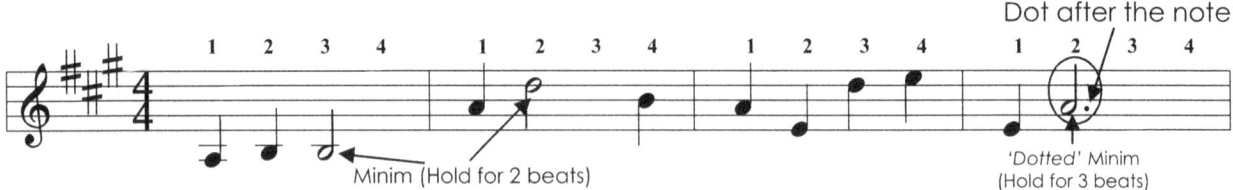

4. Read the musical notes to get familiar with the piece. Always be aware of the 'Key', to make sure you play Sharps and Flats correctly, if any.

The Key here is A Major so remember that **ALL F**'s, **C**'s and **G**'s are to be played as Sharps

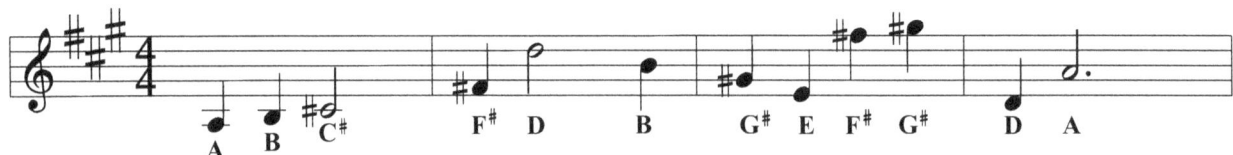

82

Playing Songs

Rock A Bye Baby
1765

Tempo - 090

84

Old MacDonald
1917

Tempo - 104

Old Mac-Do-nald had a farm, E - I - E - I O and on that farm he had some cows, E - I - E - I O. With a moo-moo here, moo-moo there, here moo, there moo, moo moo ev-ry-where, Old Mac-Do-nald had a farm, E - I - E - I O.

Love Lifted Me

James Rowe - 1912

Playing Songs

If you are ever confronted with a piece of music and you have no reference or don't remember the Key Signatures, you can use the methods below. This is the same theory of the Circle of Fourths and Fifths but in a linear view.

Always remember that **C Major** has no Sharps or Flats and there is where you will begin.

Count from the **C** note, counting **C** as number 1. Be sure to use the **C** scale and count up to the fifth note which is **G**.
G Major is the key that has 1 Sharp.

To find out which Key has 2 Sharps, count from the **G** note, counting **G** as number 1. Be sure to use the **G** scale and count up to the fifth note which is **D**.
D Major is the key that has 2 Sharps. (*Continue this method to find the others*)

Linear view of the Circle of Fifths

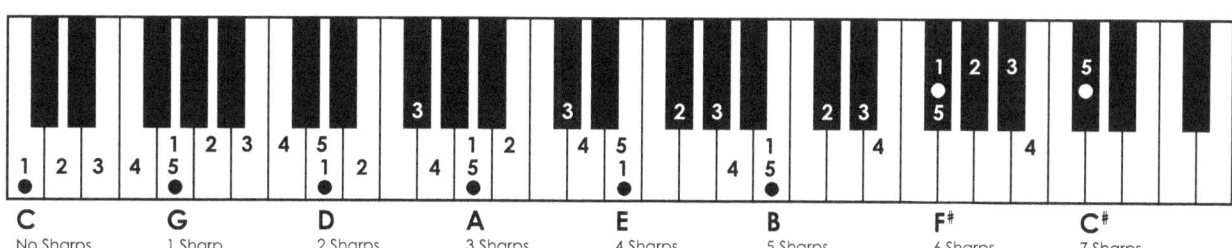

Count from the **C** note, counting **C** as number 1. Be sure to use the **C** scale and count up to the fourth note which is **F**.
F Major is the key that has 1 Flat.

To find out which Key has 2 Flats, count from the **F** note, counting **F** as number 1. Be sure to use the **F** scale and count up to the fourth note which is **B♭**.
B♭ Major is the key that has 2 Flats. (*Continue this method to find the others*)

Linear view of the Circle of Fourths

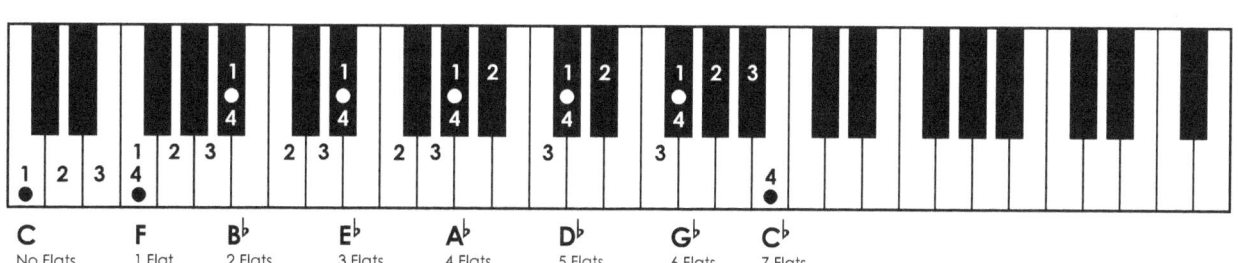

SCHEDULE

Tick the box for the day completed

Week 1
- ☐ Day 1 - **Keyboard Fam.** : White Keys (Pg 3 & 4)
- ☐ Day 2 - **Keyboard Fam.** : Black Keys (Pg 4 & 5)
- ☐ Day 3 - **Keyboard Familiarization Test** (Pg 6)
- ☐ Day 4 - **Keyboard Familiarization Test** (Pg 6)
- ☐ Day 5 - **Keyboard Familiarization Test** (Pg 6)

Week 2
- ☐ Day 1 - **Theory of Music:** The Stave, Ledger Lines
- ☐ Day 2 - **Theory of Music:** Notes & Values, Time Signatures
- ☐ Day 3 - **Theory of Music:** Dots & Ties, Key Signatures
- ☐ Day 4 - **Construction of Major Scales & Chords**: Major Scales
- ☐ Day 5 - **Construction of Major Scales & Chords**: Major Chords

Week 3
- ☐ Day 1 - **Scales, Chords & Ex. (CMaj)** : Right Hand, Left Hand
- ☐ Day 2 - **(CMaj)** : Both Hands (Ex. 3)
- ☐ Day 3 - **(CMaj)** : The Chord (Pg 20 & 21)
- ☐ Day 4 - **(CMaj)** : The Chord (Pg 22 & 23) (Ex. 1-6)
- ☐ Day 5 - **(CMaj)** : Revise and Practice all Exercises

Week 4
- ☐ Day 1 - **Scales, Chords & Ex. (GMaj)** : Right Hand, Left Hand
- ☐ Day 2 - **(GMaj)** : Both Hands (Ex. 3)
- ☐ Day 3 - **(GMaj)** : The Chord (Pg 25 & 26)
- ☐ Day 4 - **(GMaj)** : The Chord (Pg 27 & 28) (Ex. 1-6)
- ☐ Day 5 - **(GMaj)** : Revise and Practice all Exercises

Week 5
- ☐ Day 1 - **Scales, Chords & Ex. (DMaj)** : Right Hand, Left Hand
- ☐ Day 2 - **(DMaj)** : Both Hands (Ex. 3)
- ☐ Day 3 - **(DMaj)** : The Chord (Pg 30 & 31)
- ☐ Day 4 - **(DMaj)** : The Chord (Pg 32 & 33) (Ex. 1-6)
- ☐ Day 5 - **(DMaj)** : Revise and Practice all Exercises

Week 6
- ☐ Day 1 - **Scales, Chords & Ex. (AMaj)** : Right Hand, Left Hand
- ☐ Day 2 - **(AMaj)** : Both Hands (Ex. 3)
- ☐ Day 3 - **(AMaj)** : The Chord (Pg 35 & 36)
- ☐ Day 4 - **(AMaj)** : The Chord (Pg 37 & 38) (Ex. 1-6)
- ☐ Day 5 - **(AMaj)** : Revise and Practice all Exercises

Week 7
- ☐ Day 1 - **Scales, Chords & Ex. (EMaj)** : Right Hand, Left Hand
- ☐ Day 2 - **(EMaj)** : Both Hands (Ex. 3)
- ☐ Day 3 - **(EMaj)** : The Chord (Pg 40 & 41)
- ☐ Day 4 - **(EMaj)** : The Chord (Pg 42 & 43) (Ex. 1-6)
- ☐ Day 5 - **(EMaj)** : Revise and Practice all Exercises

Week 8
- ☐ Day 1 - **Scales, Chords & Ex. (BMaj)** : Right Hand, Left Hand
- ☐ Day 2 - **(BMaj)** : Both Hands (Ex. 3)
- ☐ Day 3 - **(BMaj)** : The Chord (Pg 45 & 46)
- ☐ Day 4 - **(BMaj)** : The Chord (Pg 47 & 48) (Ex. 1-6)
- ☐ Day 5 - **(BMaj)** : Revise and Practice all Exercises

Week 9
- ☐ Day 1 - **Scales, Chords & Ex. (FMaj)** : Right Hand, Left Hand
- ☐ Day 2 - **(FMaj)** : Both Hands (Ex. 3)
- ☐ Day 3 - **(FMaj)** : The Chord (Pg 50 & 51)
- ☐ Day 4 - **(FMaj)** : The Chord (Pg 52 & 53) (Ex. 1-6)
- ☐ Day 5 - **(FMaj)** : Revise and Practice all Exercises

Week 10
- ☐ Day 1 - **Scales, Chords & Ex. (B♭Maj)** : Right Hand, Left Hand
- ☐ Day 2 - **(B♭Maj)** : Both Hands (Ex. 3)
- ☐ Day 3 - **(B♭Maj)** : The Chord (Pg 55 & 56)
- ☐ Day 4 - **(B♭Maj)** : The Chord (Pg 57 & 58) (Ex. 1-6)
- ☐ Day 5 - **(B♭Maj)** : Revise and Practice all Exercises

Week 11
- ☐ Day 1 - **Scales, Chords & Ex. (E♭Maj)** : Right Hand, Left Hand
- ☐ Day 2 - **(E♭Maj)** : Both Hands (Ex. 3)
- ☐ Day 3 - **(E♭Maj)** : The Chord (Pg 60 & 61)
- ☐ Day 4 - **(E♭Maj)** : The Chord (Pg 62 & 63) (Ex. 1-6)
- ☐ Day 5 - **(E♭Maj)** : Revise and Practice all Exercises

Week 12
- ☐ Day 1 - **Scales, Chords & Ex. (A♭Maj)** : Right Hand, Left Hand
- ☐ Day 2 - **(A♭Maj)** : Both Hands (Ex. 3)
- ☐ Day 3 - **(A♭Maj)** : The Chord (Pg 65 & 66)
- ☐ Day 4 - **(A♭Maj)** : The Chord (Pg 67 & 68) (Ex. 1-6)
- ☐ Day 5 - **(A♭Maj)** : Revise and Practice all Exercises

Week 13
- ☐ Day 1 - **Scales, Chords & Ex. (D♭Maj)** : Right Hand, Left Hand
- ☐ Day 2 - **(D♭Maj)** : Both Hands (Ex. 3)
- ☐ Day 3 - **(D♭Maj)** : The Chord (Pg 70 & 71)
- ☐ Day 4 - **(D♭Maj)** : The Chord (Pg 72 & 73) (Ex. 1-6)
- ☐ Day 5 - **(D♭Maj)** : Revise and Practice all Exercises

Week 14
- ☐ Day 1 - **Scales, Chords & Ex. (G♭Maj)** : Right Hand, Left Hand
- ☐ Day 2 - **(G♭Maj)** : Both Hands (Ex. 3)
- ☐ Day 3 - **(G♭Maj)** : The Chord (Pg 75 & 76)
- ☐ Day 4 - **(G♭Maj)** : The Chord (Pg 77 & 78) (Ex. 1-6)
- ☐ Day 5 - **(G♭Maj)** : Revise and Practice all Exercises

Week 15
- ☐ Day 1 - **Families of Chords** : C, G & D (Pg 79 & 80)
- ☐ Day 2 - **Families of Chords** : A, E & B (Pg 79 & 80)
- ☐ Day 3 - **Families of Chords** : F, B♭ & E♭ (Pg 79 & 80)
- ☐ Day 4 - **Families of Chords** : A♭, D♭ & G♭ (Pg 79 & 80)
- ☐ Day 5 - **Families of Chords** : Revise and Practice

Week 16
- ☐ Day 1 - **Playing Songs** : 'Jesus Love Me' (Pg 82 & 83)
- ☐ Day 2 - **Playing Songs** : 'Rock-A-Bye Baby' (Pg 82 & 84)
- ☐ Day 3 - **Playing Songs** : 'Old MacDonald' (Pg 82 & 85)
- ☐ Day 4 - **Playing Songs** : 'Love Lifted Me' (Pg 82 & 86)
- ☐ Day 5 - **Playing Songs** : Play all four songs and read Pg 87

Congratulations, you did it!